DISCARD

The Young Adult's Guide to

PUBLIC SPEAKING

Tips, Tricks & Expert Advice for Delivering a Great Speech

without Being Nervous

THE YOUNG ADULT'S GUIDE TO PUBLIC SPEAKING: TIPS, TRICKS & EXPERT ADVICE FOR DELIVERING A GREAT SPEECH WITHOUT BEING NERVOUS

Library of Congress Cataloging-in-Publication Data

The young adult's guide to public speaking : tips, tricks & expert advice for delivering a great speech without being nervous.
        pages cm
  Includes bibliographical references and index.
   ISBN 978-1-60138-984-8 (alk. paper) -- ISBN 1-60138-984-1 (alk. paper) 1. Public speaking--Handbooks, manuals, etc. I. Atlantic Publishing Group.
   PN4129.15Y77 2015
   808.5'1--dc23
                            2015035965

Printed in the United States

Printed on Recycled Paper

Reduce. Reuse.
RECYCLE.

A decade ago, Atlantic Publishing signed the Green Press Initiative. These guidelines promote environmentally friendly practices, such as using recycled stock and vegetable-based inks, avoiding waste, choosing energy-efficient resources, and promoting a no-pulping policy. We now use 100-percent recycled stock on all our books. The results: in one year, switching to post-consumer recycled stock saved 24 mature trees, 5,000 gallons of water, the equivalent of the total energy used for one home in a year, and the equivalent of the greenhouse gases from one car driven for a year.

Over the years, we have adopted a number of dogs from rescues and shelters. First there was Bear and after he passed, Ginger and Scout. Now, we have Kira, another rescue. They have brought immense joy and love into not just into our lives, but into the lives of all who met them.

We want you to know a portion of the profits of this book will be donated in Bear, Ginger and Scout's memory to local animal shelters, parks, conservation organizations, and other individuals and nonprofit organizations in need of assistance.

– Douglas & Sherri Brown,
President & Vice-President of Atlantic Publishing

Table of Contents

"What did he say?" The Art of Communication

Public speaking is an art and a skill. An art form is something that only certain people are capable of doing — a talent that is either inherent in an individual or developed over a long period of time. A skill, on the other hand, is learned through study and experience.

Whether you are a born communicator or a newbie needing to prepare for a single presentation, this book is a tool to help you explore the basics and to provide the fundamentals of the art and skill of effective public speaking.

The fundamentals of a skill, whether it is public speaking, cooking, or basketball, are the parts of the act that anyone must consider before taking the action. In order to be an expert in one field, you must always be practicing. An example might be a basketball player that practices the skill of free throws over and over again. Shooting free throws is a fundamental part of the game that players at all experience levels need to practice on a regular basis. Likewise, a speaker must practice and keep in mind fundamentals such as diction and projection. If these speaking fundamentals are ignored, a speaker will not be understood or heard.

Every speech presentation has a singular goal: to communicate a specific thought. However, you might be asked to deliver many different types of presentations. Speeches are prepared to entertain, educate and inform. The specific goal of the presentation might differ with each speech, but they all have communication in common. Whether you are giving a toast at a wedding or participating in a class debate, you must be prepared to deliver your thoughts in a clear and concise manner.

Delivery of your speech presentation demands that you understand the art and skill of oral communication. The art of the presentation considers the creativity of your speech and the manner in which you choose to deliver the speech. The skill of the presentation demands that you put your thoughts together in a coherent manner and that you can be heard and understood as you deliver those thoughts.

Although it is possible to deliver a presentation that is short on art, it is impossible to deliver an effective presentation lacking in skill. In the same way that you cannot write an effective paper if the reader cannot read your handwriting, you cannot deliver an effective speech if the audience cannot hear or understand you.

How This Book Can Help

This book is intended to be a step-by-step manual to creating and delivering an effective speech presentation. It begins by examining a speech in its entirety and then proceeds to break the speech down into parts.

Throughout this book, you will read case studies of those who have experience in effective speech presentations. They have come to effective speech presentations down many different paths. Some of the case studies are from trained communicators, while others have developed their skills because they have expertise in other areas. Some of the individuals are naturally outgoing, and others suffer from stage fright. The one thing these individuals have in common is that they are effective communicators. They are, though, effective in different ways.

The goal of this book is to help you prepare, rehearse and ready yourself to give an effective speech presentation. It will assist you in preparing for unforeseen circumstances that might occur while you present. Every presentation you give will be different because you are communicating with different audiences (even if you are delivering the same presentation). If you have a firm grasp of the basic building blocks, you will be able to give your most effective presentation every time.

Chapter 1

Getting Your Message Across

The most important question you must ask yourself as you begin to craft your speech and continue asking yourself throughout the process of outlining, drafting, and building your entire presentation is, "What do I need to communicate?" It may be a vision, action, mission or goal. Determining what this idea is should be your first task. Without a clear vision defined from the outset, you risk wasting time and energy creating a presentation that no one cares about.

The Persuasive Speech of Patrick Henry

Patrick Henry delivered the following speech on March 23, 1775, to colonial delegates in Richmond, Virginia. The American colonies were on the brink of war with Great Britain, and Henry spoke to fellow delegates about the need to arm and defend themselves against the crown.

No man thinks more highly than I do of the patriotism, as well as abilities, of the very worthy gentlemen who have just addressed the House. But different men often see the same subject in different lights; and, therefore, I hope that it will not be thought disrespectful to those gentlemen, if, entertaining as I do opinions of a character very opposite to theirs, I shall speak forth my sentiments freely and without reserve.

This is no time for ceremony. The question before the House is one of awful moment to this country. For my own part I consider it as nothing less than a question of freedom or slavery; and in proportion to the magnitude of the subject ought to be the freedom of the debate. It is only in this way that we can hope to arrive at truth, and fulfill the great responsibility which we hold to God and our country. Should I keep back my opinions at such a time, through fear of giving offense, I should consider myself as guilty of treason towards my country, and of an act of disloyalty towards the majesty of heaven, which I revere above all earthly kings.

Mr. President, it is natural to man to indulge in the illusions of hope. We are apt to shut our eyes against a painful truth, and listen to the song of that siren, till she transforms us into beasts. Is this the part of wise men, engaged in a great and arduous struggle for liberty? Are we disposed to be of the number of those who, having eyes, see not, and having ears, hear not, the things which so nearly concern their temporal salvation?

For my part, whatever anguish of spirit it may cost, I am willing to know the whole truth — to know the worst and to provide for it. I have but one lamp by which my feet are guided; and that is the lamp of experience. I know of no way of judging of the future but by the past. And judging by the past, I wish to know what there has been in the conduct of the British ministry for the last ten years, to justify those hopes with which gentlemen have been pleased to solace themselves and the House?

Is it that insidious smile with which our petition has been lately received? Trust it not, sir; it will prove a snare to your feet. Suffer not yourselves to be betrayed with a kiss. Ask yourselves how this gracious reception of our petition comports with these war-like preparations which cover our waters and darken our land. Are fleets and armies necessary to a work of love and reconciliation? Have we shown ourselves so unwilling to be reconciled that force must be called in to win back our love? Let us not deceive ourselves, sir. These are the implements of war and subjugation — the last arguments to which kings resort. I ask gentlemen, sir, what means this martial array, if its purpose be not to force us to submission? Can gentlemen assign any other possible motives for it? Has Great Britain any enemy, in this quarter of the world, to call for all this accumulation of navies and armies?

No, sir, she has none. They are meant for us; they can be meant for no other. They are sent over to bind and rivet on us those chains which the British ministry have been so long forging. And what have we to oppose to them? Shall we try argument? Sir, we have been trying that for the last ten years. Have we anything new to offer on the subject? Nothing.

We have held the subject up in every light of which it is capable; but it has been all in vain. Shall we resort to entreaty and humble supplication? What terms shall we find which have not been already exhausted? Let us not, I beseech you, sir, deceive ourselves longer.

Sir, we have done everything that could be done to avert the storm, which is now coming on. We have petitioned; we have remonstrated; we have supplicated; we have prostrated ourselves before the throne, and have implored its interposition to arrest the tyrannical hands of the ministry and Parliament.

Our petitions have been slighted; our remonstrances have produced additional violence and insult; our supplications have been disregarded; and we have been spurned, with contempt, from the foot of the throne. In vain, after these things, may we indulge the fond hope of peace and reconciliation. There is no longer any room for hope.

If we wish to be free — if we mean to preserve inviolate those inestimable privileges for which we have been so long contending — if we mean not basely to abandon the noble struggle in which we have been so long engaged, and which we have pledged ourselves never to abandon until the glorious object of our contest shall be obtained, we must fight! I repeat it, sir, we must fight! An appeal to arms and to the God of Hosts is all that is left us!

They tell us, sir, that we are weak — unable to cope with so formidable an adversary. But when shall we be stronger? Will it be the next week, or the next year? Will it be when we are totally disarmed, and when a British guard shall be stationed in every house? Shall we gather strength by irresolution and inaction? Shall we acquire the means of effectual resistance, by lying supinely on our backs, and hugging the delusive phantom of hope, until our enemies shall have bound us hand and foot?

Sir, we are not weak, if we make a proper use of the means which the God of nature hath placed in our power. Three millions of people, armed in the holy cause of liberty, and in such a country as that which we possess, are invincible by any force which our enemy can send against us. Besides, sir, we shall not fight our battles alone. There is a just God who presides over the destinies of nations, and who will raise up friends to fight our battles for us.

The battle, sir, is not to the strong alone; it is to the vigilant, the active, the brave. Besides, sir, we have no election. If we were base enough to desire it, it is now too late to retire from the contest. There is no retreat but in submission and slavery! Our chains are forged! Their clanking may be heard on the plains of Boston! The war is inevitable — and let it come! I repeat it, sir, let it come!

It is in vain, sir, to extenuate the matter. Gentlemen may cry, "Peace! Peace!" — but there is no peace. The war is actually begun! The next gale that sweeps from the north will bring to our ears the clash of resounding arms! Our brethren are already in the field! Why stand we here idle? What is it that gentlemen wish? What would they have? Is life so dear, or peace so sweet, as to be purchased at the price of chains and slavery? Forbid it, Almighty God! I know not what course others may take; but as for me, give me liberty, or give me death!

Patrick Henry — March 23, 1775

Patrick Henry's goal in his speech was to persuade. The construction of his persuasive argument is simple, yet brilliant.

His speech was six minutes long. He spoke from his heart without notes. His speech did not need to be any longer because he had a clear vision and stated his case concisely. At the conclusion of his speech, the delegates voted on whether to fight as Henry called for, and the motion passed by a narrow margin. With this vote, Virginia joined the American Revolution against the British Crown.

Speaker's Point:
Have a clear goal in mind before you plan and write your presentation. As you continue through the steps of construction, be sure that everything you do relates directly to your intended goal.

In continuing to examine a presentation as a whole before breaking the act down into constituent parts, it is imperative that the audience be considered along with the speech. Knowing your audience is as vital to the effectiveness of your presentation as knowing what your goal is.

The Inspirational Speech of John F. Kennedy

The following speech is an excellent example of a case in which the speaker knows the audience and speaks directly to them. On June 26, 1963, U.S. President John F. Kennedy spoke to a massive crowd, estimated to be 120,000, of West Berliners at Rudolph Wilde Platz near the Berlin Wall. At the time, West Berlin was enclosed by a wall and considered a free zone within Communist East Germany.

I am proud to come to this city as the guest of your distinguished mayor, who has symbolized, throughout the world, the fighting spirit of West Berlin. And I am proud to visit the Federal Republic with your distinguished Chancellor who for so many years has committed Germany to democracy and freedom and progress, and to come here in the company of my fellow American, General Clay, who has been in this city during its great moments of crisis and will come again if ever needed.

Two thousand years ago — two thousand years ago, the proudest boast was 'civis Romanus sum.'* Today, in the world of freedom, the proudest boast is 'Ich bin ein Berliner.'**

There are many people in the world who really don't understand, or say they don't, what is the great issue between the free world and the Communist world.

> *Let them come to Berlin.*

There are some who say — there are some who say that communism is the wave of the future.

> *Let them come to Berlin.*

And there are some who say, in Europe and elsewhere, we can work with the Communists.

> *Let them come to Berlin.*

And there are even a few who say that it is true that communism is an evil system, but it permits us to make economic progress.

> *Lass' sie nach Berlin kommen.****

> *Let them come to Berlin.*

Freedom has many difficulties and democracy is not perfect. But we have never had to put a wall up to keep our people in — to prevent them from leaving us. I want to say on behalf of my countrymen who live many miles away on the other side of the Atlantic, who are far distant from you, that they take the greatest pride, that they have been able to share with you, even from a distance, the story of the last 18 years. I know of no town, no city, that has been besieged for 18 years that still lives with the vitality and the force, and the hope, and the determination of the city of West Berlin.

While the wall is the most obvious and vivid demonstration of the failures of the Communist system — for all the world to see — we take no satisfaction in it; for it is, as your Mayor has said, an offense not only against history but an offense against humanity, separating families, dividing husbands and wives and brothers and sisters, and dividing a people who wish to be joined together.

What is — What is true of this city is true of Germany: Real, lasting peace in Europe can never be assured as long as one German out of four is denied the elementary right of free men, and that is to make a free choice. In 18 years of peace and good faith, this generation of Germans has earned the right to be free, including the right to unite their families and their nation in lasting peace, with good will to all people.

You live in a defended island of freedom, but your life is part of the main. So let me ask you, as I close, to lift your eyes beyond the dangers of today, to the hopes of tomorrow, beyond the freedom merely of this city of Berlin, or your country of Germany, to the advance of freedom everywhere, beyond the wall to the day of peace with justice, beyond yourselves and ourselves to all mankind.

Freedom is indivisible, and when one man is enslaved, all are not free. When all are free, then we look — can look forward to that

> *day when this city will be joined as one and this country and this great Continent of Europe in a peaceful and hopeful globe. When that day finally comes, as it will, the people of West Berlin can take sober satisfaction in the fact that they were in the front lines for almost two decades.*
>
> *All — All free men, wherever they may live, are citizens of Berlin.*
>
> *And, therefore, as a free man, I take pride in the words 'Ich bin ein Berliner.'"*
>
> *President John F. Kennedy — June 26, 1963*

* — *"I am a Roman Citizen."*
** — *"I am a Berliner."*
*** — *"Let them come to Berlin."*

The goal of President Kennedy's speech is quite different from Patrick Henry's speech. Kennedy's goal was to show the support of the United States for the people of West Berlin. The speech Kennedy delivers to the people of West Berlin lasts for five minutes, but in that short time, Kennedy connects to the massive crowd and achieves his goal with a historic speech.

President Kennedy connects immediately with his audience by speaking of the pride he feels to be in the company of West Berlin's mayor and the chancellor of West Germany. To this opening, the crowd cheered wildly.

John F. Kennedy always will be remembered as an exceptional orator, and the speech he delivered on June 26, 1963, will be remembered as one of the most electrifying of his career. The brilliancy of this speech allowed him to achieve his goal and connect with each member of the audience and sympathetic audiences worldwide with his repeated statement, "Ich bin ein Berliner."

In some respect, Kennedy did not have to say any more than "Ich bin ein Berliner." The speech was strengthened, however, because everything he said was directly related to this sentiment.

On that day, Kennedy showed what a powerful speaker he was by knowing his audience and speaking directly to them. Had he been giving a speech with the goal to a different audience, such as the people of the United States, he would have given a different speech.

The Informational Speech of John F. Kennedy

The following is an excerpt of an address President Kennedy made to the American people on July 25, 1961.

> *Let me remind you that the fortunes of war and diplomacy left the free people of West Berlin, in 1945, 110 miles behind the Iron Curtain.*
>
> *This map makes very clear the problem that we face. The white is West Germany — the East is the area controlled by the Soviet Union and, as you can see from the chart, West Berlin is 110 miles within the area which the Soviets now dominate — which is immediately controlled by the so-called East German regime.*
>
> *We are there as a result of our victory over Nazi Germany and our basic rights to be there, deriving from that victory, include both our presence in West Berlin and the enjoyment of access across East Germany. These rights have been repeatedly confirmed and recognized in special agreements with the Soviet Union. Berlin is not a part of East Germany, but a separate territory under the control of the allied powers. Thus our rights there are clear and deep-rooted. But in addition to those rights is our commitment to sustain — and defend, if need be — the opportunity for more than two million people to determine their own future and choose their own way of life.*
>
> *Thus, our presence in West Berlin, and our access thereto, cannot be ended by any act of the Soviet government. The NATO shield was long ago extended to cover West Berlin — and we have given our word that an attack upon that city will be regarded as an attack upon us all.*

> *For West Berlin — lying exposed 110 miles inside East Germany, surrounded by Soviet troops and close to Soviet supply lines, has many roles. It is more than a showcase of liberty, a symbol, an island of freedom in a Communist sea. It is even more than a link with the Free World, a beacon of hope behind the Iron Curtain, an escape hatch for refugees.*
>
> *West Berlin is all of that. But above all it has now become — as never before — the great testing place of Western courage and will, a focal point where our solemn commitments stretching back over the years since 1945, and Soviet ambitions now meet in basic confrontation.*
>
> *It would be a mistake for others to look upon Berlin, because of its location, as a tempting target. The United States is there; the United Kingdom and France are there; the pledge of NATO is there — and the people of Berlin are there. It is as secure, in that sense, as the rest of us — for we cannot separate its safety from our own."*
>
> *President John F. Kennedy*
> *in a televised address to the American people*
> *on July 25, 1961*

The goal of the two speeches was similar: to garner support for the U.S. position in West Berlin. The speeches were different in tone because they were delivered to different audiences. It is important, though, that as you consider your presentation, you see that the audience is just as important as the message.

'Come, we shall have some fun now!' thought Alice. 'I'm glad they've begun asking riddles. — I believe I can guess that,' she added aloud.

`Do you mean that you think you can find out the answer to it?' said the March Hare.

`Exactly so,' said Alice.

`Then you should say what you mean,' the March Hare went on.

'I do,' Alice hastily replied; 'at least — at least I mean what I say — that's the same thing, you know.'

`Not the same thing a bit!' said the Hatter. 'You might just as well say that "I see what I eat" is the same thing as "I eat what I see!"'

'You might just as well say,' added the March Hare, 'that "I like what I get" is the same thing as "I get what I like!"'

'You might just as well say,' added the Dormouse, who seemed to be talking in his sleep, `that "I breathe when I sleep" is the same thing as "I sleep when I breathe!"'

'It IS the same thing with you,' said the Hatter, and here the conversation dropped, and the party sat silent for a minute…

Lewis Carroll,
Alice's Adventures in Wonderland, 1865

As you consider the message and audience of a particular speech, ask yourself a more complex question, "Did the speaker mean what he said?" In the case of Alice's conversation at the Mad Hatter's tea party, ask, "Did the speaker say what he meant?" The Mad Hatter and the March Hare prove that these two things are not always the same.

In examining these two complicated questions, you encounter one of the most baffling issues of human communication. Sometimes you can think you are being clear on a point, and you say what you mean and mean what you say, but the point is totally misinterpreted by the listener. Why is this?

A number of factors are at play here. Go back to the first two examples of speeches presented above, and ask yourself if the speakers, Patrick Henry and John F. Kennedy, said what they meant. What you are looking for is whether the speakers were clear in their vision and whether they were able to construct their speeches in such a way as to clearly present those visions to their audiences. Again, you must consider the intent of the speech and the intended audience.

A Congratulatory "Thank You" Delivered by George W. Bush

An example of a speech delivered by a president that has caused controversy because of the way different audiences received it is a speech that President George W. Bush delivered on May 1, 2003. On this day, President Bush landed on the deck of the aircraft carrier USS Abraham Lincoln and spoke to the crew of the carrier as well as the people of the United States in this televised address. President Bush spoke from a podium on the deck of the carrier under a banner that read, "Mission Accomplished."

Admiral Kelly, Captain Card, officers and sailors of the USS Abraham Lincoln, my fellow Americans: Major combat operations in Iraq have ended. In the Battle of Iraq, the United States and our allies have prevailed. And now our coalition is engaged in securing and reconstructing that country.

In this battle, we have fought for the cause of liberty and for the peace of the world. Our nation and our coalition are proud of this accomplishment — yet it is you, the members of the United States military, who achieved it. Your courage — your willingness to face danger for your country and for each other — made this day possible. Because of you, our nation is more secure. Because of you, the tyrant has fallen, and Iraq is free.

Operation Iraqi Freedom was carried out with a combination of precision, and speed, and boldness the enemy did not expect, and the world had not seen before. From distant bases or ships at sea, we sent planes and missiles that could destroy an enemy division or strike a single bunker. Marines and soldiers charged to Baghdad across 350 miles of hostile ground, in one of the swiftest advances of heavy arms in history. You have shown the world the skill and the might of the American Armed Forces.

This nation thanks all of the members of our coalition who joined in a noble cause. We thank the Armed Forces of the United Kingdom, Australia, and Poland, who shared in the hardships of war. We thank all of the citizens of Iraq who welcomed our troops and joined in the liberation of their own country. And tonight, I have a special word for Secretary Rumsfeld, for General Franks, and for all the men and women who wear the uniform of the United States: America is grateful for a job well done.

The character of our military through history — the daring of Normandy, the fierce courage of Iwo Jima, the decency and idealism that turned enemies into allies — is fully present in this generation. When Iraqi civilians looked into the faces of our servicemen and women, they saw strength, and kindness, and good will. When I look at the members of the United States military, I see the best of our country, and I am honored to be your commander in chief.

In the images of fallen statues, we have witnessed the arrival of a new era. For a hundred years of war, culminating in the nuclear age, military technology was designed and deployed to inflict casualties on an ever-growing scale. In defeating Nazi Germany and imperial Japan, Allied Forces destroyed entire cities, while enemy leaders who started the conflict were safe until the final days. Military power was used to end a regime by breaking a nation. Today, we have the greater power to free a nation by breaking a dangerous and aggressive regime. With new tactics and precision weapons, we can achieve military objectives without directing violence against civilians. No device of man can remove the tragedy from war. Yet it is a great advance when the guilty have far more to fear from war than the innocent.

In the images of celebrating Iraqis, we have also seen the ageless appeal of human freedom. Decades of lies and intimidation could not make the Iraqi people love their oppressors or desire their own enslavement. Men and women in every culture need liberty like they need food, and water, and air. Everywhere that freedom arrives, humanity rejoices. And everywhere that freedom stirs, let tyrants fear.

We have difficult work to do in Iraq. We are bringing order to parts of that country that remain dangerous. We are pursuing and finding leaders of the old regime, who will be held to account for their crimes. We have begun the search for hidden chemical and biological weapons, and already know of hundreds of sites that will be investigated. We are helping to rebuild Iraq, where the dictator built palaces for himself, instead of hospitals and schools. And we will stand with the new leaders of Iraq as they establish a government of, by, and for the Iraqi people. The transition from dictatorship to democracy will take time, but it is worth every effort. Our coalition will stay until our work is done. And then we will leave — and we will leave behind a free Iraq.

The Battle of Iraq is one victory in a war on terror that began on September the 11th, 2001, and still goes on. That terrible morning, 19 evil men — the shock troops of a hateful ideology — gave America and the civilized world a glimpse of their ambitions. They imagined, in the words of one terrorist, that September the 11th would be the "beginning of the end of America." By seeking to turn our cities into killing fields, terrorists and their allies believed that they could destroy this nation's resolve, and force our retreat from the world. They have failed.

In the Battle of Afghanistan, we destroyed the Taliban, many terrorists, and the camps where they trained. We continue to help the Afghan people lay roads, restore hospitals, and educate all of their children. Yet we also have dangerous work to complete. As I speak, a special operations task force, led by the 82nd Airborne, is on the trail of the terrorists, and those who seek to undermine the free government of Afghanistan. America and our coalition will finish what we have begun.

From Pakistan to the Philippines to the Horn of Africa, we are hunting down al-Qaeda killers. Nineteen months ago, I pledged that the terrorists would not escape the patient justice of the United States. And as of tonight, nearly one-half of al-Qaeda's senior operatives have been captured or killed.

The liberation of Iraq is a crucial advance in the campaign against terror. We have removed an ally of al-Qaeda, and cut off a source of terrorist funding. And this much is certain: No terrorist network will gain weapons of mass destruction from the Iraqi regime, because the regime is no more.

In these 19 months that changed the world, our actions have been focused, and deliberate, and proportionate to the offense. We have not forgotten the victims of September the 11th — the last phone calls, the cold murder of children, the searches in the rubble. With those attacks, the terrorists and their supporters declared war on the United States. And war is what they got.

Our war against terror is proceeding according to principles that I have made clear to all:

Any person involved in committing or planning terrorist attacks against the American people becomes an enemy of this country, and a target of American justice.

Any person, organization, or government that supports, protects, or harbors terrorists is complicit in the murder of the innocent, and equally guilty of terrorist crimes.

Any outlaw regime that has ties to terrorist groups, and seeks or possesses weapons of mass destruction, is a grave danger to the civilized world, and will be confronted.

And anyone in the world, including the Arab world, who works and sacrifices for freedom has a loyal friend in the United States of America.

Our commitment to liberty is America's tradition — declared at our founding, affirmed in Franklin Roosevelt's Four Freedoms, asserted in the Truman Doctrine, and in Ronald Reagan's challenge to an evil empire. We are committed to freedom in Afghanistan, in Iraq, and in a peaceful Palestine. The advance of freedom is the surest strategy to undermine the appeal of terror in the world.

Where freedom takes hold, hatred gives way to hope. When freedom takes hold, men and women turn to the peaceful pursuit of a better life. American values, and American interests, lead in the same direction: We stand for human liberty.

The United States upholds these principles of security and freedom in many ways — with all the tools of diplomacy, law enforcement, intelligence, and finance. We are working with a broad coalition of nations that understand the threat, and our shared responsibility to meet it. The use of force has been, and remains, our last resort. Yet all can know, friend and foe alike, that our nation has a mission: We will answer threats to our security, and we will defend the peace.

Our mission continues. Al-Qaeda is wounded, not destroyed. The scattered cells of the terrorist network still operate in many nations, and we know from daily intelligence that they continue to plot against free people. The proliferation of deadly weapons remains a serious danger. The enemies of freedom are not idle, and neither are we. Our government has taken unprecedented measures to defend the homeland — and we will continue to hunt down the enemy before he can strike.

The war on terror is not over, yet it is not endless. We do not know the day of final victory, but we have seen the turning of the tide. No act of the terrorists will change our purpose, or weaken our resolve, or alter their fate. Their cause is lost. Free nations will press on to victory.

Other nations in history have fought in foreign lands and remained to occupy and exploit. Americans, following a battle, want nothing more than to return home. And that is your direction tonight. After service in the Afghan and Iraqi theaters of war — after 100,000 miles, on the longest carrier deployment in recent history — you are homeward bound. Some of you will see new family members for the first time — 150 babies were born while their fathers were on the Lincoln. Your families are proud of you, and your nation will welcome you.

We are mindful as well that some good men and women are not making the journey home. One of those who fell, Corporal Jason Mileo, spoke to his parents five days before his death. Jason's father said, "He called us from the center of Baghdad, not to brag, but to tell us he loved us. Our son was a soldier." Every name, every life, is a loss to our military, to our nation, and to the loved ones who grieve. There is no homecoming for these families. Yet we pray, in God's time, their reunion will come.

Those we lost were last seen on duty. Their final act on this earth was to fight a great evil, and bring liberty to others. All of you — all in this generation of our military — have taken up the highest calling of history. You are defending your country, and protecting the innocent from harm. And wherever you go, you carry a message of hope — a message that is ancient, and ever new. In the words of the prophet Isaiah: "To the captives, 'Come out!' and to those in darkness, 'Be free!'"

Thank you for serving our country and our cause. May God bless you all, and may God continue to bless America.

President George W. Bush — May 1, 2003

President Bush's speech on this day has become known as his "Mission Accomplished" speech, primarily because of the large banner that hung above him on the USS Lincoln as he spoke. With this statement, it would be easy to think this was the intended message of his speech. In some respect, this would be a correct assertion. The mission accomplished on this day, though, did not refer to the mission in Iraq or Afghanistan, but instead referred to the mission of the crew of the USS Lincoln that had just been deployed for 11 months and was on its way home.

President Bush's problem was that his address was for those on the deck of the aircraft carrier and for a nationwide television audience that saw "Mission Accomplished" and heard that "Major combat operations in Iraq have ended." However, later in the speech, President Bush says, "The war on terror is not over."

President Bush's message to the crew of the USS Lincoln might have been clear, but his message to the American people was confusing. It is easy to wonder what "Mission Accomplished" meant to the American television viewer that day. In light of history, we know that this is not what happened. He might have meant they had ended for the crew of the USS Lincoln.

Compare President Bush's speech to Patrick Henry's on March 23, 1775, and you will discover many similarities. Both speeches were made to underline an ongoing struggle with a foreign power. Henry's speech was made to move the listener to action, and President Bush spoke to thank those who had taken action.

The difference between the speeches is that Patrick Henry's speech was crystal clear in its meaning, while President Bush's speech was not clear enough to be fully understood. While Henry spoke to a divided audience — an audience that did not fully agree with his point of view — he delivered a message in which he meant what he said and said what he meant. It is only speculation, but one might think that President Bush would change a few things about his "Mission Accomplished" address considering the scope of the audience to which he was speaking.

After he delivered his speech, a member of President Bush's staff told reporters that the press had mischaracterized the President's intended message. The goal of speaking to the public should always be to deliver a clear message that leaves little room for mischaracterization. The speeches presented earlier in the chapter by Patrick Henry and President John F. Kennedy leave almost no room for mischaracterization.

Speakers and Speeches

As a speaker, you might be asked to deliver many types of presentations. Likewise, there are many professions in which being able to deliver an effective speech presentation is vital to the success of the job. A list of those individuals that benefit from being able to deliver an effective speech include:

- Teachers
- Sales professionals
- Politicians
- Company executives
- Coaches
- Church leaders
- Lawyers
- Students

This list can get longer. Anyone who has to be able to clearly deliver information, motivate, persuade, inspire, or entertain groups of people will benefit by knowing the essential building blocks of delivering an effective presentation.

Each of the professions noted above are called on to deliver a variety of presentation types. In the speech examples offered earlier in this chapter, you read a persuasive speech delivered by

Patrick Henry, an inspirational and informative speech delivered by John F. Kennedy, and congratulatory thanks offered by George W. Bush. These are only three of the many types of speech presentations you might be asked to give.

Types of speeches

Acceptance — A speech delivered on receiving an award or gift. An acceptance speech is often a "thank you" for the award and thanks to those that supported or assisted in the work.

After Dinner — A speech that is often entertaining in nature but might also be any one of the other speeches. An after-dinner speech is connected directly to the group at hand.

Demonstration — A presentation that, as the name implies, demonstrates a product, idea or theory

Graduation — Various types of graduation speeches exist, such as valedictorian speeches that exceptional students deliver. These speeches are congratulatory motivational speeches.

Informative — A presentation in which specific information must be delivered clearly

Persuasive — A presentation meant to persuade the listeners to adopt a particular point of view. A debate is a good example of a type of persuasive presentation.

Presenting Awards/Gift — A speech that will call on the speaker to talk about the receiver of the award/gift and what was done to receive the award/gift

Toast — A toast can take many forms but is delivered in recognition of an individual or event.

Many of the speeches defined above often go beyond what might be termed a speech. In fact, many speeches might be better defined as presentations. A demonstration or an informative speech might include elements beyond the speaker at the podium. These elements might include a PowerPoint®, slides, films and other tools used to help the speaker make a clearer presentation. Keeping that in mind, the term presentation will be used to identify speeches that might employ additional tools that aid the speech. These tools will be examined later in this book.

Clarity is the key to an effective speech. In striving for clarity, it is imperative that you take all aspects of your presentation into account. Know your message. Know your goal. Know your audience. Know what will make up the complete package of your presentation.

In the coming chapters, presentations are broken down to their component parts, and each aspect of an effective presentation is explored. You will learn each step of the process including clarifying your vision, drafting your speech, using helpful presentation tools and overcoming a fear of presenting. This book will also teach you how to understand the space you will be working in, and how to handle audience questions and feedback.

After you examine the structure of a presentation and build your own, you will be able to say clearly with confidence, "Mission accomplished."

Chapter 2

The Building Blocks of a Good Presentation

> "Let's start at the very beginning
> A very good place to start..."
>
> Oscar Hammerstein II —
> *The Sound of Music*

Start by deconstructing and identifying the parts of your presentation. Do not think about the final product at this point. Think about what your presentation can be. Be open to all the possibilities. Unless you have been called on to deliver a simple toast or welcoming speech (and those will be covered later on in this book), think now about the full scope and all the possibilities you have as you begin to craft your presentation.

The building blocks of an effective presentation include:

- The message
- The audience
- The research
- The writing
- Auxiliary tools
- Practice
- The setting
- Preparing to deliver
- The delivery
- Feedback

This chapter will explore each of these building blocks and how you can use them to craft an effective presentation. It is meant only to give an overview of each of these essential building blocks. Subsequent chapters will explore each item more thoroughly.

The Message

Whether you are preparing to write a speech, a novel, or a Broadway musical, you must start at the beginning by identifying what you are writing about. When you consider the subject of your presentation, you start by identifying your message.

What is my message? This heavy question might be the most important question you answer in your quest to create an effective presentation. Being able to answer this question in a clear, concise manner will help you craft your presentation and will tell your audience that you know what you are about. This is your mission statement, your goal, your action. It has many words to identify it. To you, it is your guiding light.

The most important building block of any presentation is the mission statement. You need to be able to state your business. A mission statement defines what your presentation is about.

You should be able to define your mission in one simple sentence. It is well worth your time and effort to work on your mission statement until it is perfect — that is, when it clearly and concisely defines your purpose. When someone can read it quickly and know what your focus is without you having to clarify it, add something to it, or answer any questions, your mission statement will be complete.

The importance of a mission statement can be compared to the importance of a plot in a good story. In literature, a writer might refer to the mission as a plot, or more simply, as an action. You can tell when you are reading a book or watching a movie with a good plot. If someone asks you what the story is about, you can explain it easily. On the other hand, think about the movies you have seen that have no plot or one that is poorly defined. The characters might be good, and the movie might have been beautifully filmed, but if there is no plot, the movie fails. The same can be said of your presentation. If you cannot state what your goal is, you cannot hope to make an audience understand your message.

The mission statement

To teach you how to prepare a presentation, you can refer to the following model. A community health initiative that you're doing for the organization you volunteer with is your model. This initiative focuses on the obesity epidemic and children's health. The children's health initiative is called Teach a Kid to Fish (TKF). **The mission of TKF is to prevent and reduce childhood obesity**

by empowering Lincoln children and families to eat healthy food and be active. The active verbs in this mission are to prevent and reduce.

The presentation will engage in the task of introducing this community health initiative to a local organization and address the issue of children's health as it relates to the mission of the organization. If you had to create this presentation, you would start by considering the mission of the organization: **to prevent and reduce childhood obesity by empowering Lincoln children and families to eat healthy and be active.** You also might consider the organizational vision: **TKF envisions creating community solutions for children's health.**

As you begin to craft your presentation, everything you say and present to introduce your group to this organization should be directly related to these statements of mission and vision.

Beyond the mission and vision statements, also think about what you want your audience to take away from your presentation. You have an organizational goal but also have a goal in mind for your presentation.

For this model, the goal is to make the audience aware of the organization, its mission, vision and how it relates to the community. The presentation might have several additional goals such as requesting donations to support the cause, seeking other volunteers and getting attendees to sign on to the mailing list or follow social media. All these additional goals, however, are directly related to the primary mission and vision of the organization and the goal of the presentation: to make the audience aware of the organization.

Speaker's Point:
You might be aware of a short and to-the-point presentation that is known as an elevator pitch. This type of presentation is much like a 30-second television commercial in its nature. The gist of an elevator pitch is being able to state your case in the time it takes an elevator to travel four floors. To begin thinking about constructing such as an elevator pitch, you can go back, look at your mission statement, and ask yourself, "What is the most concise way I can sum up my goal?"

For those other types of presentations you might have the opportunity to deliver, whether it is an acceptance speech, the introduction of an award winner, or an oral project presentation, the same idea holds true as it is described above: Know what your message is and what you want your audience to take away from your presentation.

If your assignment is to introduce an individual of note to a group of students, your goal is fairly simple: Identify the individual and, perhaps, welcome him or her.

Example: Suppose that Patrick Henry was invited to speak to a your school, and you have been asked to introduce him. Your goal has been stated in the supposition above: **to introduce**. You also must consider the fact that Mr. Henry is an invited guest and should be welcomed. This is your starting point.

You can simply say, "I'd like to welcome Mr. Patrick Henry, who has come today to talk to us." Although this is true, it does not tell the listeners who Patrick Henry is and why he is speaking. The question for the presenter now becomes, "What is the best way to introduce and welcome Patrick Henry?"

This simple task will become the second presentation model as you proceed through this book.

Speaker's Point:

Before you do anything in the way of crafting a presentation, sit down at your computer or with a pen and paper and note your goals. Make your statements as simple as possible and in as few words as possible. Make the primary components of your statements active verbs.

The Audience

Now that you have defined what message you will deliver and what the goal of your presentation is going to be, take a close look at the audience to which you will be making your presentation. Although you can deliver the same message to a wide variety of audiences, the manner in which you deliver it can vary to make the biggest possible impact.

If you go back and look at the speeches in Chapter 1 and consider the audiences they were aimed at, you can get a good idea as to how effective each of the presentations were and how they might have had a different effect on different audiences. John F. Kennedy's speeches, in particular, are a good case to study for the same message delivered in a different manner to differing audiences. President George W. Bush's "Mission Accomplished" speech is also a good example of how different audiences might react to the same speech.

Considering your audience and the manner in which you deliver your message is a vital building block in the development of an effective presentation. Knowing your audience can make all the difference in whether your presentation is a success or a failure.

In the TKF model set forth earlier in this chapter, the organization was invited to make a presentation to a community group. The group asked that the organization introduce itself to its members. So, if you were in charge of making this presentation, you need to know a little bit about the particular organization before deciding on the manner of the presentation.

A community group could mean a local parent teacher organization at an elementary school that will be predominately young moms. A community group could also mean a group of students from different schools in your county. Although the message you deliver to the two groups might be the same, you would be wise to explore the specifics of your audience fully. If you are talking about children's health to a group of young parents, your focus is on how parents can work to ensure their children are the healthiest they can be. The parents understand the importance and reasons they need to keep their children healthy. On the other hand, the message about children's health to a group of students might be about their individual choices and their family's choices.

There are times when you might need to deliver your presentation to a mixed audience, and you should be prepared to do this as well. The community group in question above might be a neighborhood organization gathering where you could expect to speak to the young mom, her family, and students. The presenter should be prepared to face all possible audiences.

On the other hand, there will be those presentations designed for and delivered to a singular audience. Presenters who deliver information of a highly technical nature intended for a highly select audience do not need to consider how their presentations will be received by varying audiences.

The model that was put forth earlier in the chapter that required an introduction of Patrick Henry to a group of students is a specific request, so you know you will have to make your introduction interesting. Even though you are speaking to a group of students, you need to consider the differences of each school that you introduce Patrick Henry to. For example, you should know whether all the students speak the same language. Ask yourself if the introduction should be offered in Spanish or sign language. Find out about the student population. Is it an all-girl school perhaps?

Everything you can find out about the audience to whom you will be speaking will make your presentation better. If you go into a presentation with a generic speech prepared for a generic audience, you run a greater risk of boring people, speaking down to them, speaking over their heads or, depending on the subject matter of your presentation, speaking counter to specific beliefs such as political beliefs, religious values or lifestyle choices.

If you have been asked to speak to a group you are not familiar with, you might ask a number of questions to help you mold your presentation:

- How large will the audience be?

- What is the purpose of the organization to which I am speaking?

- What will the makeup of the audience be?

- Why is the organization interested in hearing about this topic?

- Are there specific areas of this topic that should be avoided? Why?

You are asked to deliver a speech, whether it is a short introduction or a longer presentation, for a specific purpose. You have a message to convey. Knowing your audience is a vital building block to delivering an effective presentation.

The Research

Another key building block of an effective presentation is knowing how to back your information up. You must be sure of your facts. Whether you are delivering a presentation about the epidemic of childhood obesity or introducing Patrick Henry, any time you state what you believe to be a fact, be ready to back it up. You might be asked about it during the question-and-answer segment of your presentation.

It would not go over well for the introduction of Patrick Henry to say, "He played wide receiver for the New England Patriots and caught 15 touchdown passes last season." You could make that statement if it were clearly a joke, but to say something like that to a group of students about your guest without backing it up is not a good idea. Look into well-regarded history books and get good information. "Patrick Henry is considered to be a Founding Father of the United States and served as governor of Virginia from 1776 to 1778 and in 1784. His famous words 'Give me liberty or give me death' moved Virginia to revolution." These facts can be backed up.

Knowing and trusting your facts is just as important as knowing your audience. Do your homework before you prepare your presentation, and the prep work will go smoother.

Writing

Even if you plan to deliver your presentation without notes or note cards, sit down and draft an entire presentation, if not, at least an outline. An outline is a way to get an idea about the direction of your presentation. Not all presentations, such as debates, will benefit from a point-by-point outline. Some presentations are best prepared for by noting the facts on a series of index cards or other tools that are easily rearranged.

Writing involves bringing all your knowledge, notes, and research together to shape the information you have into an effective presentation. By writing, you will first see what works and what does not work in your presentation. Writing your thoughts down into a singular piece that flows in an orderly fashion from one thought to the next will help you clarify your message.

Auxiliary Tools

In creating your presentation, you have many tools at hand to deliver your message in a more creative, clear and effective way. Auxiliary tools such as PowerPoint, slide shows and video can help define and underscore points that you want or need to make.

The danger with any auxiliary tools is that a presenter might come to rely too much on them. Do not fall into this trap. Use auxiliary tools only when they best serve your ultimate goal.

Think of the presentations you have seen in which a presenter has used a PowerPoint presentation to help deliver a message. As the PowerPoint was shown, the presenter reads the copy on each of the slides word for word. In this case, one of the tools was unnecessary. Either the presenter was not needed, or the PowerPoint was not needed. When presenters choose to read slides word for word, the PowerPoint takes away from the speaker's goal. Use a tool only when it helps make your task easier.

When you employ any of the many auxiliary tools at your disposal to make your message clearer, you are helping yourself and your audience. Auxiliary tools, if used correctly, can make your presentation clearer and much more engaging.

Also, you do not need to use any tools beyond your own ability to write and speak. Let your message and goal guide you. Trust your ability to deliver your message simply. Use auxiliary tools only to strengthen and clarify.

Practice

There is an old joke that involves tourists on the street in Manhattan who ask the question, "How do you get to Carnegie Hall?" The native New Yorker answers, "Practice." The same holds true for delivering an effective presentation. The advice is true for those who are new to delivering presentations and for those who have done it many times, especially if they are developing a new presentation. Practice makes perfect.

Practice is important for those who are new to delivering presentations because it can:

- Help develop confidence
- Facilitate the understanding of how to better use the voice
- Assist in learning to address an audience
- Help clarify the intended message
- Aid in understanding how to employ auxiliary presentation tools

Practice is important for those who are good presenters because it can:

- Help keep presentation skills sharp
- Aid in improving the presentation
- Help eliminate any bad presentation habits

Whether you develop a presentation to deliver one time or you develop multiple presentations that you will deliver many times, practicing is essential to making your presentation as effective as it can be.

The one aspect of practicing to deliver a speech that is equally as important to new speakers as it is to more experienced presenters is preparing your voice. Knowing how to use your voice to be heard and to deliver desired effects is a vital aspect of practice and preparation for presentation. Your voice is an essential building block to an effective presentation.

Stage fright is a common phobia. A well-practiced presenter has taken the first step toward conquering stage fright.

The Setting

Knowing where you will be making your presentation and understanding how to effectively work in the space is just as important as knowing who your audience will be. Being prepared to speak in a small classroom-type space and then being faced with an auditorium can throw a large wrench into any speaker's plans. You, in the end, need to be able to adapt to whatever comes your way. You also must recognize the importance of making your presentation fit the environment.

The variety of settings in which you could possibly make a presentation is huge, from the elevator speech described earlier that could be delivered in an actual elevator, to an auditorium filled with 1,500 people, to a rowdy school cafeteria. If you are making a single presentation, it is easy to learn the complete details of your setting. If you are developing a presentation to make to multiple audiences, give thought as to how to develop a presentation that can easily be adjusted from elevator to auditorium.

Consider the invitation to introduce Patrick Henry to an audience of school students. You have asked all the questions regarding the makeup of the audience, but think about the variety of spaces you might encounter at a school:

- Classroom
- Gym
- Cafeteria
- Auditorium
- Hallway
- Library

Each of these locations presents different opportunities to connect with your audience as well as different challenges. If your introduction includes a slide show on the life of Patrick Henry, and you find yourself being asked to do your presentation in a classroom where there is no projection screen, you might need to alter your plans.

Know your audience. Know your setting. Knowing what you are walking into will help you make a more effective presentation.

Preparing to Deliver

Preparing to deliver your presentation refers to the time you spend just before delivering your speech checking to make sure that everything is in place. The everything refers to your notes, PowerPoint presentation, microphone, your voice and your energy level.

Preparing to deliver is running through a checklist of systems that you will develop to make sure everything is in place when you need to call on it to make your presentation as effective as possible.

Think about that automatic checklist you mentally run through every day as you prepare to leave the house in the morning. "Are my lights in my room off? Do I have my keys? Do I have my backpack? Are my gym clothes in my bag?" Everyone has that checklist.

When the microphone does come on, your voice will need to be warmed up and ready. If the microphone does not come on, your voice will need to be even more warmed up and ready. Vocal warm-ups should always be a part of your presentation preparation.

It is at this point that those who suffer from stage fright can take the second step toward conquering that fear. Knowing that you are well prepared will help you to be more confident in yourself and your presentation.

The Delivery

There you are standing confidently in front of 800 people with a clear and focused presentation, but your task is not yet complete. You are introduced, and the spotlight shines on you. There are a number of things to think about as you deliver your speech, some of which you should be prepared to deal with but that are difficult to practice.

- Energy
- Timing
- Awareness
- Listening to your audience

You will experience a level of energy when you step onto the stage that you will not have encountered as you rehearsed your presentation. There are ways to use this energy for your own purposes that will make your presentation come alive.

One of the good things about stage fright is that it creates nervous energy that can be harnessed and channeled for the good of your presentation.

You will find that the timing of your presentation is something else that is difficult to determine in a rehearsal. There are reasons for this. Your energy level is different. The size and energy of the audience will be a relative unknown.

Taking a reading on the state of your audience is also a way of connecting with your audience early on in your presentation. Connecting with your audience and holding their attention demand that you have a continuous awareness of your audience. An effective speech is more about talking with your audience as opposed to talking at them.

To talk with your audience, you need to be able to listen to them. An effective conversation demands that you listen and speak. You will be doing all or most of the speaking, but your audience is not silent by any means. You need to be able to listen to them as you speak.

Feedback

When your presentation is complete and the audience is applauding, you are not yet done. The feedback you receive from your audience is important. If you have been listening to your audience during your presentation, you have been taking in feedback. The applause you are hearing after your presentation is feedback. The question and answer session you hold after your presentation is complete is feedback. Your personal conversation with your host is feedback. The information you get from all of these feedback sources will help as you refine your presentation and/or your presentation techniques.

Whether you are looking to strengthen a particular presentation or looking to strengthen your abilities as a speaker, feedback you receive from every audience you encounter can be used to help make you a more effective presenter.

Each step of the building blocks of putting together an effective oral presentation have been broadly described and defined. The chapters that follow will speak to each step in greater detail, but it is here that the entire process has been broken down and outlined with the pieces laid out in front of you. These are the fundamental elements of effective public speaking. The only component that has not been addressed is experience.

Experience

Experience, like the energy you get from the delivery of a live presentation, (as opposed to a rehearsal or practice) can be acquired only through doing it. There are ways to experience making presentations without going through all the steps as described above.

To get the experience and practice of speaking in public and of making public statements, you can attend and plan to be vocal at club meetings such as key club meetings, student government gatherings and even community clubs such as book groups at libraries. Many of these venues will be free of charge and will offer you the opportunities to gain experience in speaking to groups. Many of these opportunities will give the experience in speaking in an impromptu manner. You also might find opportunities to speak where a little preparation will be called for.

Speaker's Point:

The definition of an impromptu presentation is that it is one done without any previous preparation. This can be wholly true, but most often there is some amount of preparation done on several of the building blocks as listed above. An effective impromptu speaker can prepare by knowing the audience, having some knowledge and/or background on the subject matter, speaking with an awareness of the surroundings, being vocally prepared to speak and speaking while listening to the audience.

Now that you have viewed the act of the living oral presentation as a complete package and disassembled it into its component parts, it is time to take a closer look at each of these components.

Chapter 3

The Message and the Audience

" *he medium is the message,*
therefore the audience is the content."

Marshall McLuhan

You might have heard the first part of the quote above, but it is the second part of the quote, "… therefore the audience is the content," that speaks volumes about how you, as a speaker, relate to your audience. The meaning of the quote changes considerably when you consider it an entire thought as opposed to a half thought, "The medium is the message…" The idea that the audience is the content could mean that each member of your audience will supply their own interpretation of what your message is. When you are speaking in a live presentation, you are the medium. You are the message.

Abraham Lincoln's Message

"Four score and seven years ago our fathers brought forth on this continent, a new nation, conceived in Liberty, and dedicated to the proposition that all men are created equal.

Now we are engaged in a great civil war, testing whether that nation, or any nation so conceived and so dedicated, can long endure. We are met on a great battlefield of that war. We have come to dedicate a portion of that field, as a final resting place for those who here gave their lives that that nation might live. It is altogether fitting and proper that we should do this.

But, in a larger sense, we can not dedicate — we can not consecrate — we can not hallow — this ground. The brave men, living and dead, who struggled here, have consecrated it, far above our poor power to add or detract. The world will little note, nor long remember what we say here, but it can never forget what they did here. It is for us the living, rather, to be dedicated here to the unfinished work which they who fought here have thus far so nobly advanced. It is rather for us to be here dedicated to the great task remaining before us — that from these honored dead we take increased devotion to that cause for which they gave the last full measure of devotion — that we here highly resolve that these dead shall not have died in vain — that this nation, under God, shall have a new birth of freedom — and that government of the people, by the people, for the people, shall not perish from the earth."

Abraham Lincoln — Gettysburg Address — Nov. 19, 1863

The Gettysburg Address is considered one of the most memorable speeches in American history, and Abraham Lincoln is widely thought to be one of the most thoughtful presidents and an excellent orator.

President Lincoln was called to Gettysburg to dedicate the Soldier's National Cemetery in Gettysburg, Pennsylvania. Five months before this address, Union forces had defeated Confederate forces at the Battle of Gettysburg. In 1863, the United States was in the midst of a most divisive and bloody Civil War.

It is always interesting to study presidential speeches because the audience a president must speak to is so vast. In chapter 1, you read three different presidential addresses that were crafted to specific audiences, yet broadcast to audiences worldwide. If you consider these addresses in the terms of Marshall McLuhan's quote at the beginning of this chapter, the potential content of each of the speeches might be unfathomable.

In crafting and delivering the Gettysburg Address, President Lincoln had intended his audience to be the American people. Because of the communications restrictions of the time, only the estimated 15,000 to 20,000 people present at the ceremony heard the address. Lincoln's speech was also available in following days in newspapers around the country.

To say that Lincoln's words were meant as an address to the American people of that time is to say that he was speaking to "a house divided against itself." Thus, the interpretation of Lincoln's words and the content of the speech varied among regions.

Lincoln's message was crystal clear, but some of the embedded statements could have been considered upsetting to those who did not share his particular convictions. "... the audience is the content."

What is Your Message?

"... the audience is the content."

With this is mind, you begin the process of crafting your presentation by finely focusing on your message and your goal. Craft whatever presentation you plan to present knowing that 20 different people will receive it in 20 different ways.

Ask yourself the questions:

- What is my message?
- What is the goal of my presentation?
- What do I want the audience to take away from my speech?

These are the most difficult questions you will face in your preparation, especially if you are preparing a presentation that will be delivered to variable audiences. Think back to the "Mission Accomplished" speech of President George W. Bush. He might have had a strong notion as to what his message was and the goal of his speech, but what the variable audience took away from the presentation called into question the presentation's preparation.

Consider the two models explored in chapter 2. One of the models, TKF, poses a complex presentational challenge. The second model, the introduction of Patrick Henry, is rather simple.

To start building a presentation for TKF, first consider the givens:

- The mission and vision of the organization is **to prevent and reduce childhood obesity by empowering Lincoln children and families to eat healthy and be active. TKF envisions creating community solutions for children's health.**

- The goal of the presentation is to introduce the organization to a group that has invited the organization to make a presentation.

- The audience is the PTO (Parent Teacher Organization) of a local public elementary school.

These three facts will be the starting point of creating a presentation. Before proceeding with putting more definition to this presentation, it is instructive to consider some variables that might occur in the future as the organization creates a presentation that it can use to deliver its message to a variety of audiences.

In creating a presentation frame that can be used at elementary schools, TKF can focus on its mission/vision statement and on the goal of introducing the organization to groups that ask it to make such presentations. The variable is the audience. The audience is the content.

The organization's message will be the same for each presentation when asked to introduce the organization to an audience. If the organization receives an invitation to speak to a group with the aim of introducing itself, the goal is clear. It is the task of the presenter to tailor the presentation to the audience.

Some presentations will demand that you tailor your message to the audience. You read an example of this in chapter 1 in

President John F. Kennedy's two speeches regarding the support of the United States for the people of West Germany in the early 1960s. To appeal to the two different audiences, though, Kennedy had to widen the scope of the message for the people of the United States. The speech he delivered to the people of West Germany spoke specifically of and directly to them. The message he delivered to the people of the United States spoke of the wider threat of communism worldwide.

President Kennedy succeeded in defining what he wanted his audience to take away from his two speeches. Kennedy wanted the people of West Germany and the people of the United States to understand that the United States stood against communism and stood for the people and governments that it considered its allies in the fight against communism. President Kennedy's audiences for each of those presentations were the people of West Germany and the United States and the governments opposed to the ideals for which the United States stands. Kennedy sent the same message to the world — a message that was crystal clear but interpreted in a different way in Moscow than it was in somewhere like Minnesota.

TKF must decide and define what it wants the audience of the parent teacher organization meeting to take away from its presentation. This variable might change with each presentation. Though the message "to prevent and reduce childhood obesity by empowering Lincoln children and families to eat healthy and be active" might stay the same with each presentation, the definition of what the organization wants the audience to take away from the presentation might vary.

Parents and teachers of students will interpret the message of TKF differently than will a group of students. Students might be interested in learning about the issue of childhood obesity, but they will respond to the message in a different way. The difference in this audience will affect the way the presentation is made.

The question now becomes how you tailor your presentation to your audience. The answer is in how you define the audience you are speaking to and what their specific issues are. In the stated model, the audience will be parents, teachers, and several young students. Because the presentation is at an elementary school, the parents are those of young children between the ages of five and 11 years old. There might be a few grandparents or other caregivers in the audience. The group also will include some elementary school teachers who regularly have to deal with children who might be affected by the issue of obesity and the many health problems it presents.

When the invitation to speak was made, the presenter might have asked the following questions to define the audience further:

- Do you worry about your child's/student's weight/ health?

- Does the school provide information about neighborhood resources for nutrition and physical activity?

- What, if any, are the barriers that make it difficult to feed your child healthy foods and to be physically active?

- Does your child walk to school? If not, explain what barriers exist that make it so your child does not walk to school?

- What do you feel is the role of schools in the childhood obesity epidemic? Who would you like to receive information regarding your child's weight status, nutrition, and physical activity habits?

Several simple questions like these can help the presenter further define the audience and help get the conversation started after the presentation.

Speaker's Point:

When you receive an invitation to present, do not be shy about asking as many questions as you need to clarify your role as a presenter and the situation into which you will be entering. Any information you can gather can help you make your presentation as effective as possible. The more you know about your audience, the easier it will be to get your message across.

You might be able to gather as much information about your audience as is humanly possible, but you must know that there always will be those in the audience who will not get your message, be offended by your message, disagree with your message, misinterpret your message or be bored by your message. Know that you cannot control many of these impressions. Instead, you can use these negative impressions as opportunities to help further define your message.

Some messages will have more potential for misinterpretation or disagreement than others. When there is a reasonable potential for conflict, consider tailoring your presentation to your message, such as creating your presentation with the understanding that there will be those in the audience who will disagree with you, will not understand your message, or might misinterpret your message no matter how clearly you present it.

Creating a presentation to introduce audiences to TKF might seem like there could not be anyone who would disagree with the message regarding children's health. However, add the word obesity in the message, and you suddenly might find that you get some push back. Creating a presentation that introduces an audience to an organization with the mission, **"to empower Lincoln children and families to eat healthy and be active. TKF envisions creating community solutions for children's health"** is one thing. Again, you cannot argue with children's health. What makes the mission and message of TKF somewhat difficult is the inclusion of the word obesity.

In dealing with messages that are often difficult, a presenter needs to create a presentation that gets the message across in such a way that it does not turn the audience off. You can tailor your presentation to fit your message and your audience.

Dealing with the obesity epidemic is a great example. Go back to the intended audience for the TKF presentation. If the presentation is made to 100 parents, teachers, and children, statistics say that about 30 percent of the audience is going to be overweight or obese. While TKF should not shy away from its mission statement, it does no good to point a finger at parents who might be overweight or obese about the health consequences related to their overweight and obese children. The intention of the presentation is not to shame the parents and their children. It is to introduce the audience to an organization that is trying to create community solutions for children's health.

Beyond the fact that the audience probably has a good number of parents who suffer from the consequences of being overweight and obese, a number of individuals in the audience probably consider the political implications of the obesity epidemic. A segment of the population does not agree with many of the opinions of those engaged in the struggle to prevent obesity because of tax and governmental control issues. The question is probably not so much about children's health as it is about the perceived hot-button issue of obesity.

The question for TKF then becomes how to stay truthful to its mission and message and at the same time keep channels of communication open to those who perceive the discussion of obesity as a potentially insulting or politically charged issue. To achieve this, must deliver a message that is compassionate, understanding and contains an awareness of the full scope of the message and its audience.

To achieve this goal, the presenter must have a firm understanding of its message, its audience and what it wants its audience to take away from the presentation. In this case, the presenter wants the audience to know that TKF is an organization that seeks to create community solutions for children's health. The organization does not want the audience to leave feeling that the organization thinks that they are bad parents if their children are overweight or that they think a tax on sugar-sweetened beverages will put an end to the obesity epidemic in the country.

If, in the introduction of the organization to the particular audience, they can start a community discussion as to what the community can do to better the health of the children of the community, the organization will have achieved its goal.

The second model that was described is the simple matter of introducing Patrick Henry to a student audience. To do this, the presenter has three simple goals:

- Welcome Patrick Henry.
- Thank Patrick Henry.
- Give the students background on Patrick Henry.

This list is not necessarily the order in which the described tasks need to be presented but is a checklist of what needs to happen as the speaker prepares his or her presentation. Sometimes, the most difficult thing about making a presentation is keeping it simple.

Language and Tone

No matter what you are speaking about, begin with the simplest message possible. In other words, as you start to craft your presentation, you should boil your mission/message down to a crystal of an idea. As you proceed, make sure everything you include in your presentation, no matter how complex, directly relates to that crystal of an idea.

Keeping that in mind, make sure that the language and tone of your presentation remain true to your audience. It does no good to speak in terms your audience won't understand. Do not skip over technical facts thinking that your audience will not understand them. The words you choose and the way you speak them are vital to the effectiveness of your presentation.

On Feb. 5, 2003, U.S. Secretary of State Colin Powell addressed the Security Council of the United Nations regarding Iraq's failure to disarm. What follows is a portion of Secretary Powell's presentation.

Mr. President, Mr. Secretary General, distinguished colleagues, I would like to begin by expressing my thanks for the special effort that each of you made to be here today.

This is important day for us all as we review the situation with respect to Iraq and its disarmament obligations under UN Security Council resolution 1441.

Last November 8, this council passed resolution 1441 by a unanimous vote. The purpose of that resolution was to disarm Iraq of its weapons of mass destruction. Iraq had already been found guilty of material breach of its obligations, stretching back over 16 previous resolutions and 12 years.

Resolution 1441 was not dealing with an innocent party, but a regime this council has repeatedly convicted over the years. Resolution 1441 gave Iraq one last chance, one last chance to come into compliance or to face serious consequences. No council member present in voting on that day had any illusions about the nature and intent of the resolution or what serious consequences meant if Iraq did not comply.

And to assist in its disarmament, we called on Iraq to cooperate with returning inspectors from Unmovic and IAEA.

We laid down tough standards for Iraq to meet to allow the inspectors to do their job.

This council placed the burden on Iraq to comply and disarm and not on the inspectors to find that which Iraq has gone out of its way to conceal for so long. Inspectors are inspectors; they are not detectives.

I asked for this session today for two purposes: first, to support the core assessments made by Dr. Blix and Dr. El-Baradei. As Dr. Blix reported to this council on January 27: 'Iraq appears not to have come to a genuine acceptance, not even today, of the disarmament which was demanded of it.'

And as Dr. El-Baradei reported, Iraq's declaration of December 7: 'Did not provide any new information relevant to certain questions that have been outstanding since 1998.'

My second purpose today is to provide you with additional information, to share with you what the United States knows about Iraq's weapons of mass destruction as well as Iraq's involvement in terrorism, which is also the subject of resolution 1441 and other earlier resolutions.

I might add at this point that we are providing all relevant information we can to the inspection teams for them to do their work.

The material I will present to you comes from a variety of sources. Some are U.S. sources. And some are those of other countries.

Some of the sources are technical, such as intercepted telephone conversations and photos taken by satellites. Other sources are people who have risked their lives to let the world know what Saddam Hussein is really up to.

I cannot tell you everything that we know. But what I can share with you, when combined with what all of us have learned over the years, is deeply troubling.

What you will see is an accumulation of facts and disturbing patterns of behavior. The facts on Iraqis' behavior — Iraq's behavior demonstrate that Saddam Hussein and his regime have made no effort — no effort — to disarm as required by the international community. Indeed, the facts and Iraq's behavior show that Saddam Hussein and his regime are concealing their efforts to produce more weapons of mass destruction.

Colin Powell — Feb. 5, 2003

In this example, Secretary Powell's tone is extremely serious, and his language is stark and to the point. There is no question as to what his goal is. The full version of this speech is technical in nature, as Powell shows satellite images of what he defines as Iraq's concealment of weapons. The tone of this speech can be described as deathly serious. It would have been a mistake for Powell to speak lightly of this or to joke about it in any manner. It also would have been ineffective to simply say that Iraq was developing weapons of mass destruction without having some technical proof of the allegation.

A Final Point About Message and Audience

The final point to be made as you think about message and audience and about what you want your audience to take away from your presentation is that of your role as a presenter. The individual who presents Patrick Henry to an audience must create the presentation and keep in mind that he or she is not the featured speaker. His or her role is to present another speaker. The individual asked to introduce TKF to an audience must consider the fact that the presentation is not about her or him but about the organization. That is not to say that either of these presenters should not put any of their personality into the presentation, but the goal is the organization or the featured speaker.

There will be more information about the speaker's role later this book. It is important, though, that as you begin to develop your message, your goal, and how it will be presented to your specific audience, you keep in mind the role you are playing in the presentation as a whole. Your role and why you are speaking are good first steps in the research you will do to make your presentation as effective as it can be.

Chapter 4

The Research

efore the writing takes place, the presenter needs to know and understand why he or she has been asked to speak, what information he or she is expected to present, and what information he or she might need to learn before putting the presentation together. The presenter will determine whether the presentation should reflect several different points of view and how to incorporate those various viewpoints. In short, this chapter will explore the kinds of research that might need to be done before the actual writing of the presentation and the presenting of information to an audience. Giving a presentation is similar to writing a paper, and facts should back up any information. The chapter will discuss how to present certain types of factual information, how to present information as opinion, and how to footnote information presented as facts.

Ronald Reagan's Provocative Speech

Here is a portion of a most memorable speech Ronald Reagan made at the Brandenburg Gate, Berlin Wall on June 12, 1987. This is an example of a speech presented by a speaker that understands why he has been asked to speak, understands the message he is delivering and the audience he is delivering it to. It embodies a specific point of view and offers a good mix of fact and opinion.

Thank you very much. Chancellor Kohl, Governing Mayor Diepgen, ladies and gentlemen: Twenty-four years ago, President John F. Kennedy visited Berlin, speaking to the people of this city and the world at the city hall. Well, since then two other presidents have come, each in his turn, to Berlin. And today I, myself, make my second visit to your city.

We come to Berlin, we American presidents, because it's our duty to speak, in this place, of freedom. But I must confess, we're drawn here by other things as well: by the feeling of history in this city, more than 500 years older than our own nation; by the beauty of the Grunewald and the Tiergarten; most of all, by your courage and determination. Perhaps the composer, Paul Lincke, understood something about American presidents. You see, like so many presidents before me, I come here today because wherever I go, whatever I do: Ich hab noch einen koffer in Berlin. [I still have a suitcase in Berlin.]

Our gathering today is being broadcast throughout Western Europe and North America. I understand that it is being seen and heard as well in the East. To those listening throughout Eastern Europe, I extend my warmest greetings and the good will of the American people. To those listening in East Berlin, a special word: Although I cannot be with you, I address my remarks to you just as surely as to those standing here before me. For I join you, as I join your fellow countrymen in the West, in this firm, this unalterable belief: Es gibt nur ein Berlin. [There is only one Berlin.]

Behind me stands a wall that encircles the free sectors of this city, part of a vast system of barriers that divides the entire continent of Europe. From the Baltic, south, those barriers cut across Germany in a gash of barbed wire, concrete, dog runs, and guard towers. Farther south, there may be no visible, no obvious wall. But there remain armed guards and checkpoints all the same — still a restriction on the right to travel, still an instrument to impose upon ordinary men and women the will of a totalitarian state. Yet it is here in Berlin where the wall emerges most clearly; here, cutting across your city, where the news photo and the television screen have imprinted this brutal division of a continent upon the mind of the world. Standing before the Brandenburg Gate, every man is a German, separated from his fellow men. Every man is a Berliner, forced to look upon a scar.

Where four decades ago there was rubble, today in West Berlin there is the greatest industrial output of any city in Germany — busy office blocks, fine homes and apartments, proud avenues, and the spreading lawns of parkland. Where a city's culture seemed to have been destroyed, today there are two great universities, orchestras and an opera, countless theaters, and museums. Where there was want, today there's abundance — food, clothing, automobiles — the wonderful goods of the Ku'damm. From devastation, from utter ruin, you Berliners have, in freedom, rebuilt a city that once again ranks as one of the greatest on Earth. The Soviets may have had other plans. But, my friends, there were a few things the Soviets didn't count on Berliner herz, Berliner humor, ja, und Berliner schnauze. [Berliner heart, Berliner humor, yes, and a Berliner schnauze.] [Laughter]

In the 1950s, Khrushchev predicted: 'We will bury you.' But in the West today, we see a free world that has achieved a level of prosperity and well being unprecedented in all human history. In the Communist world, we see failure, technological backwardness, declining standards of health, even want of the most basic kind — too little food. Even today, the Soviet Union still cannot feed itself. After these four decades, then, there stands before the entire world one great and inescapable conclusion: Freedom leads to prosperity. Freedom replaces the ancient hatreds among the nations with comity and peace. Freedom is the victor.

And now the Soviets themselves may, in a limited way, be coming to understand the importance of freedom. We hear much from Moscow about a new policy of reform and openness. Some political prisoners have been released. Certain foreign news broadcasts are no longer being jammed. Some economic enterprises have been permitted to operate with greater freedom from state control. Are these the beginnings of profound changes in the Soviet state? Or are they token gestures, intended to raise false hopes in the West, or to strengthen the Soviet system without changing it? We welcome change and openness; for we believe that freedom and security go together, that the advance of human liberty can only strengthen the cause of world peace.

There is one sign the Soviets can make that would be unmistakable, that would advance dramatically the cause of freedom and peace. General Secretary Gorbachev, if you seek peace, if you seek prosperity for the Soviet Union and Eastern Europe, if you seek liberalization: Come here to this gate! Mr. Gorbachev, open this gate! Mr. Gorbachev, tear down this wall!

In the Philippines, in South and Central America, democracy has been given a rebirth. Throughout the Pacific, free markets are working miracle after miracle of economic growth.

In the industrialized nations, a technological revolution is taking place — a revolution marked by rapid, dramatic advances in computers and telecommunications.

In Europe, only one nation and those it controls refuse to join the community of freedom. Yet in this age of redoubled economic growth, of information and innovation, the Soviet Union faces a choice: It must make fundamental changes, or it will become obsolete. Today thus represents a moment of hope. We in the West stand ready to cooperate with the East to promote true openness, to break down barriers that separate people, to create a safer, freer world.

And surely there is no better place than Berlin, the meeting place of East and West, to make a start. Free people of Berlin: Today, as in the past, the United States stands for the strict observance and full implementation of all parts of the Four Power Agreement of 1971. Let us use this occasion, the 750th anniversary of this city, to usher in a new era, to seek a still fuller, richer life for the Berlin of the future. Together, let us maintain and develop the ties between the Federal Republic and the Western sectors of Berlin, which is permitted by the 1971 agreement.

And I invite Mr. Gorbachev: Let us work to bring the Eastern and Western parts of the city closer together, so that all the inhabitants of all Berlin can enjoy the benefits that come with life in one of the great cities of the world. To open Berlin still further to all Europe, East and West, let us expand the vital air access to this city, finding ways of making commercial air service to Berlin more convenient, more comfortable, and more economical. We look to the day when West Berlin can become one of the chief aviation hubs in all central Europe.

One final proposal, one close to my heart: Sport represents a source of enjoyment and ennoblement, and you many have noted that the Republic of Korea — South Korea — has offered to permit certain events of the 1988 Olympics to take place in the North. International sports competitions of all kinds could take place in both parts of this city. And what better way to demonstrate to the world the openness of this city than to offer in some future year to hold the Olympic games here in Berlin, East and West?

In these four decades, as I have said, you Berliners have built a great city. You've done so in spite of threats — the Soviet attempts to impose the East-mark, the blockade. Today the city thrives in spite of the challenges implicit in the very presence of this wall. What keeps you here? Certainly there's a great deal to be said for your fortitude, for your defiant courage. But I believe there's something deeper, something that involves Berlin's whole look and feel and way of life — not mere sentiment. No one could live long in Berlin without being completely disabused of illusions. Something instead, that has seen the difficulties of life in Berlin but chose to accept them, that continues to build this good and proud city in contrast to a surrounding totalitarian presence that refuses to release human energies or aspirations. Something that speaks with a powerful voice of affirmation, that says yes to this city, yes to the future, yes to freedom. In a word, I would submit that what keeps you in Berlin is love — love both profound and abiding.

Perhaps this gets to the root of the matter, to the most fundamental distinction of all between East and West. The totalitarian world produces backwardness because it does such violence to the spirit, thwarting the human impulse to create, to enjoy, to worship. The totalitarian world finds even symbols of love and of worship an affront. Years ago, before the East Germans began rebuilding their churches, they erected a secular structure:

the television tower at Alexander Platz. Virtually ever since, the authorities have been working to correct what they view as the tower's one major flaw, treating the glass sphere at the top with paints and chemicals of every kind. Yet even today when the sun strikes that sphere — that sphere that towers over all Berlin — the light makes the sign of the cross. There in Berlin, like the city itself, symbols of love, symbols of worship, cannot be suppressed.

As I looked out a moment ago from the Reichstag, that embodiment of German unity, I noticed words crudely spray-painted upon the wall, perhaps by a young Berliner, 'This wall will fall. Beliefs become reality.' Yes, across Europe, this wall will fall. For it cannot withstand faith; it cannot withstand truth. The wall cannot withstand freedom.

And I would like, before I close, to say one word. I have read, and I have been questioned since I've been here about certain demonstrations against my coming. And I would like to say just one thing, and to those who demonstrate so. I wonder if they have ever asked themselves that if they should have the kind of government they apparently seek, no one would ever be able to do what they're doing again.

Thank you and God bless you all.

Ronald Wilson Reagan — June 12, 1987

This will long be remembered as one of Ronald Reagan's best speeches. The speech is a good example at this point in the book because it presents a wide variety of facts, opinions, statements, others' points of view and visions for a future, all to state one clear goal.

This is an interesting speech to examine because it has a nearly identical goal as that put forth by President John F. Kennedy 24 years earlier. This message to the people of Berlin was that the United States stood with them in their quest for freedom. President Reagan's speech to the people of Germany and to the people of the world is every bit as memorable and effective as President Kennedy's.

Like the speeches delivered by most modern presidents, Ronald Reagan's speech at the Brandenburg Gate, Berlin Wall on June 12, 1987, was written by a member of the presidential speechwriting team, Peter Robinson. As a presidential speechwriter, Robinson had to make sure that the facts embedded in the speech were accurate, and he had to prepare a speech that was true to the individual who would be delivering the speech. In this case, it was Ronald Reagan.

An excellent article about the development of this speech is on the National Archives website at **www.archives.gov/publications/ prologue/2007/summer/berlin.html**.

In this article, Robinson describes how he prepared to write the speech, researched the facts of the speech and researched what the tone of the speech should be.

Historical facts

As a presidential speechwriter, Peter Robinson had access to many tools and sources to identify and verify facts. Many of the facts cited in this speech are easily verifiable facts and are nicely embedded so it does not sound like he is just reading off statistics.

When a fact is delivered, you should be able to provide a reputable source. If, in your search of fact confirmation, you discover a difference of opinion on a specific fact, you should note that in your speech. To not do so can be a cause for confusion and disagreement. The use of well-researched and verifiable facts can help to clarify a speech. The use of information that is not true or that has not been confirmed will work to make things unclear or cause disagreement. Often, speakers use wrong information in order to persuade or to achieve a specific goal. However, if you want your audience to trust you and to truly persuade those who disagree, always make sure your facts can be backed up with research.

When Nikita Krushchev said, "We will bury you," he spoke it as a point of fact, but it was merely an opinion that even he had to clarify later when many Westerners believed it was a reference to nuclear war. Krushchev said later that the Soviet Union would bury the west economically. He also clarified by saying on Aug. 24, 1963, "I once said, 'We will bury you,' and I got into trouble with it. Of course, we will not bury you with a shovel. Your own working class will bury you."

Speaker's Point:

Several speeches have been used as examples in this text in which the speaker has employed the use of a foreign language to make a point. Most famous is John F. Kennedy's statement *"Ich bin ein Berliner."* There is an urban legend that relates that in saying this, what Kennedy said was, "I am a jelly doughnut." Though this is an amusing story, this is not the case. The phrase translates literally to "I am one with Berliners" and has become "I am a Berliner." The reason for the urban legend is that a Berliner is a type of jelly doughnut. The legend rose out of the fact that Kennedy spoke the line with an American accent heavy with east coast/Boston accent. In preparing for this speech, Kennedy did his research and worked with an individual that coached him on proper pronunciation.

Identifying Facts

In preparing the presentation on childhood obesity for Teach a Kid to Fish (TKF), it is vital that the speaker defines and clearly describes the issue with well-researched facts. Just saying childhood obesity is a problem is not as compelling as backing that claim up with facts.

To spell out the facts and inform the listener where the facts come from is important to making a clear case.

"As obesity rates have increased dramatically over the last 30 years in the United States in adults and children, obesity has become a national epidemic. Data from the Centers for Disease Control and Prevention (CDC) from 2003-2004 and 2005-2006 indicated that two-thirds of U.S. adults were either obese or overweight. Based on representative samples of U.S. children, nationally one-third of children are overweight or obese. According to the esteemed Robert Wood Johnson Foundation, we are raising the first generation of youth who will live sicker and shorter lives than their parents. The childhood obesity epidemic has become a public health emergency with tripling of prevalence rates since 1980. According to a recent report published by Trust for America's Health, Nebraska ranks as having the 21st highest percent of obese and overweight children in the United States, with 31.5 percent of Nebraska children measured as obese or overweight. The childhood obesity epidemic disproportionately affects children who are minority, live in poverty or live in neighborhoods without access to healthy foods and safe play spaces. These disparities are demonstrated nationally and in our community.

Consortium to Lower Obesity in Chicago Children (CLOCC) posted a report from Trust for America's Health's 'Bending the Obesity Cost Curve' that stated reducing obesity rates by 5 percent could lead to more than $29 billion in health care savings in five years. Imagine the impact 5 percent could have on health-related cost for employers.

Although 5 percent doesn't sound like much, what would that look like for Nebraska? The report found that in five years, the country would save $29.8 billion, $158.1 billion in ten years, and a staggering $611.7 billion in 20 years. We only are talking 5 percent. National Collaborative on Childhood Obesity Research estimates the direct medical spending for obesity per Nebraskan is predicted to increase to $642 per person in 2013 and $1,486 per person by 2018 if current trends continue. This will increase state level obesity costs from $823 million per year for the state in 2013 to \$1.919 billion per year for the state by 2018. If 2008 obesity prevalence could be held steady until 2018 (no increase, no decrease), savings for the state are estimated at \$1.07 billion per year."

The facts related in this example are interesting on several different levels:

- They spell out the rapid growth of the epidemic of childhood obesity.
- They define the economic impact of the growing epidemic.
- All the facts are delivered with the source of the facts.

The delivery of facts with reputable source references in the presentation makes for a more compelling presentation. Comparing the delivery of the facts regarding childhood obesity above to the statement delivered by Ronald Reagan in the previous example shows that facts supported by reputable source references are always more compelling.

Be Sure of Your Sources

Identifying good sources is key to being certain the information you deliver to your listeners is solid. What counts as a "good source" will vary depending on what you are speaking about. In the example provided above, the cited sources from the CDC, Robert Wood Johnson Foundation, Trust for America's Health, and National Collaborative on Childhood Obesity Research are all highly respected sources of information regarding health and health care.

Even if the speaker is a recognized expert on the topic he or she is speaking about, it is important that the facts put forward are verifiable. Having verified facts will help boost your credibility on your topic and get your readers to trust what you have to say.

It is possible that a speaker, while presenting well-researched facts, also might offer opinions on the studies presented. The opinions offered might not agree with the facts. If opinions are offered, it should be stated that the opinions expressed are the opinions of the speaker. In contrast, a speaker may offer opinions that differ from his/her own opinions or from the facts. Again, if this is done, it should be stated clearly that opinions are just that, opinions.

Presenting opinions or facts that are in opposition to your own point of view can be a good way of keeping an audience engaged in the speech and help to generate questions in a post-presentation question and answer session. Remember, your goal is not only to present fact, instruct, etc., but also to hold the interest of the audience. Presenting opposing viewpoints can be a great way to do this as long as they are well researched.

If the speaker of the presentation on childhood obesity had delivered the following presentation, the case might not have been quite as compelling:

"As obesity rates have increased dramatically over the past 30 years in the United States in adults and children, obesity has become a national epidemic. Data from Wikipedia indicated that two-thirds of U.S. adults were either obese or overweight. Based on representative samples of U.S. children, nationally one-third of children are overweight or obese. According to an article in the *Reader's Digest*, we are raising the first generation of youth who will live sicker and shorter lives than their parents.

The childhood obesity epidemic has become a public health emergency with tripling of prevalence rates since 1980. According to a recent report published by *US Magazine*, Nebraska ranks as having the 21st highest percent of obese and overweight children in the United States, with 31.5 percent of Nebraska children measured as obese or overweight. The childhood obesity epidemic disproportionately affects children who are minority, live in poverty or live in neighborhoods without access to healthy foods and safe play spaces. These disparities are demonstrated nationally and in our community."

In the example above, all the numbers are the same as in the previous example, but the sources cited have been changed. Wikipedia, *Reader's Digest*, and *US Magazine* might have gotten their facts and information from the CDC, Robert Wood Johnson Foundation, Trust for America's Health, and National Collaborative on Childhood Obesity Research, but they are not as respected or as trustworthy as the original source.

Whenever you can, go to the original source. If you cannot go to the original source, be sure to find evidence where multiple sources cite similar figures. Remember Ronald Reagan's citing Berlin as being more than 500 years older than the United States. Although it was impossible to cite the specific date of the founding of the city of Berlin, many sources cited approximate dates of the origins of the German city. Also, Reagan's reference to the age difference was not so specific that somebody could say he was wrong. His reference stated, *"But I must confess, we're drawn here by other things as well: by the feeling of history in this city, more than 500 years older than our own nation ..."*

Research helps you before you move on to the next step of writing your presentation. Before the writing takes place, the presenter needs to know and understand why he or she has been asked to speak, what information he or she is expected to present, and what information he or she might need to learn before putting the presentation together. The presenter will determine whether the presentation should reflect several different points of view, and if so, how to incorporate those various viewpoints. In short, research is the work that will need to be done before the actual writing of the presentation.

Although it might be assumed that the presenter has been asked to offer views and opinions on certain subjects due to expertise, giving a presentation is much the same as writing a paper, and information put forth should be backed up by facts. Knowing the facts and where and how those facts were derived will help the speaker answer questions that will arise during a post-presentation question and answer session. Doing your research and knowing your material back and forth as well as being familiar with the opposing opinions and opposing facts will help you understand the complex dynamics of the subject matter and underline your expertise.

Being able to understand and communicate the various viewpoints of a given subject can help in delivering a clear presentation. Knowing the various viewpoints also can help calm the nerves of even the most hesitant presenter. Once you know your facts and are able to back them up, you are ready to write your speech presentation.

Chapter 5

The Writing

T he research is done. You know what you will be speaking about and why. You have a firm grasp on the message you wish to deliver, so now you can focus on the how.

This chapter will guide you through the outlining of the presentation and a draft-by-draft exploration of the writing process. The word process is a step-by-step procedure of organizing your thoughts in a thorough outline that will then guide in the writing of the first draft of the presentation. The three basic parts of the presentation — the opening, the presentation main body, and the closing — will be described, and a variety of speech types will be explored to demonstrate the organizational process fully. The chapter will describe how the presentation will go from a loose first draft to a finely tuned final draft that incorporates notes and descriptions of all supplemental messaging tools.

It is in this chapter that you also will tackle the issue of whether to memorize the presentation because this will have some influence on the writing process. Often, if an individual is extremely familiar with the material, he or she need not take the writing of the presentation past the outline stage. The chapter will end by exploring several types of non-traditional presentation formats such as improvised question and answer sessions, impromptu presentations, multi-party discussions/debates/presentations and how best to be prepared.

The Outline

The outline is the guide you will use as a road map to your writing, or if you choose not to go past the outline stage, the delivery of your speech presentation. Outlines can serve numerous functions in the writing process.

- Organizing thoughts — The primary function of an outline, whether you are using it as a writing tool or as a tool from which to speak, is to organize your thoughts. An outline is not meant to be a word-for-word text of your presentation, so you will construct your outline by noting the flow of your speech in a point-by-point manner and covering the major points of the speech and each of the minor points that go with the major points.

- Directional guides — The outline also serves as a road map to your presentation as it helps you get a good sense of the flow of the presentation from the beginning, middle and end. After you have constructed your outline and before you sit down to write your speech, you will be able to see all the covered points and understand how each point leads to the next.

- Brainstorming tools — Last but not least, the outline is a tool to help you brainstorm your full presentation. Being able to lay out all your potential presentation points is a wonderful way to make sure you have included everything you need to include to make your presentation as effective as it can be.

The outline is the tool you can use to put everything on the table, change it, lay it out differently and change it up yet again. You will give yourself ample time to edit your presentation later. Once you are done with your outline, the writing will be much easier because you will have a step-by-step instruction manual that you created.

Writing the outline

Writing an outline for your speech is like to writing an outline for an essay in school. The only difference is you will be able to think a little more visually about your essay, and you can use visual clues and behaviors to help you get across your point.

You can start the thinking about your outline much the same way you would an essay. Begin by collecting all of the information you know from your research and the message you want to get across to your listeners. You then can begin to brainstorm any way you like. A common way is to begin writing your outline.

To structure the flow of your outline, start by going back to the primary mission statement you created. Everything in your outline and presentation should have a direct relation to that statement. Proceed by noting the primary ideas you would like to get across. These primary ideas will make up the main points of your outline. These can be compared to the topic sentences in a research essay.

Once you have noted the main outline points, you can continue by noting, beneath each of the main points, ideas and points that are related to the main points. These ideas may include stories that support the main point or support the point or opposing opinions related to the point. Your first outline draft is the best place to put it all out on paper. That is, note everything that you might possibly include in your presentation by doing a brain-storming session with yourself. You will have the opportunity later to choose what is most relevant to your presentation.

These main points and sub-points will make up the body of your outline. Beyond this, you will determine a proper opening statement as well as a closing statement that wraps up your presentation.

Begin to think about preparing your presentation in three main sections: opening, main body and closing. Each of the sections serves a function.

You will introduce yourself to your audience in the opening of your presentation. You also will have to engage your audience's interest in the subject of your speech in the opening. How you choose to open will depend on your subject matter and your personality.

The most important goal of your opening is to create a bond with your audience. Creating a bond with an audience can be as simple as standing out from behind the podium, smiling, looking directly at your audience and introducing yourself. Thank the audience immediately for the invitation. Relate a common interest. *More information about opening and creating a bond with your audience will be in Chapter 10.*

The main body of your presentation is where you will get to the business of your speech. In the example of TKF, the object of the presentation is to introduce the audience to the organization and its mission.

The closing of the speech will depend on what your goals are. Here you will make a call to action, bring any loose ends together, and summarize your presentation. The closing is the place where you do what you need to do to ensure your presentation's goals are met.

In determining how to open your presentation, start by thinking about your audience and as yourself. Depending on your audience, your opening may vary. You might choose to begin by telling a joke or a funny story related to your topic. You could to cite a startling statistic such as, "According to the esteemed Robert Wood Johnson Foundation, we are raising the first generation of youth who will live sicker and shorter lives than their parents."

Likewise, your subject and your audience should determine your closing comments. You might choose a call to action, a wrap-up of the information you have just delivered or a humorous anecdote.

Although the body of your speech contains the most pertinent information for your audience, the introduction and conclusion of your speech will require the most thought and creativity on your part. The introduction must get the audience's attention from the start. It is their first look at you as a speaker, and once they make their impressions of your presentation, it is hard to change their minds. The conclusion also must leave a lasting impression on them, as it is the last thing they will remember about your speech. You want to end on a strong statement or a strong note. For that reason, many persuasive speeches end with a call to action. Tell your audience what they should go forth and do. For an informative presentation, end your speech much as you would a research paper: Sum up your main points and perhaps look to the future for a powerful ending.

Outline example

There are many different styles of outlines. The two most basic outline types are topic outlines and sentence outlines. In a topic outline, you will use one or several words as point references to guide you through your writing. In sentence outlines, each point of your guide is expressed as a statement. In each of these forms, the structure is presented as a major point and minor point skeleton structure. The points are divided using Roman numerals, capital letters, numbers and lowercase letters to indicate how the point falls into the skeleton structure of major point and a subdivision of that point.

Topic Outline Example:

The topic of this speech outline is to introduce the audience to Teach a Kid to Fish, a community organization committed to fighting the childhood obesity epidemic that you volunteer for. The audience is the Parent Teacher Organization of a local school.

I. Introduction
   A. Myself
      1. Background
      2. Involvement at organization
   B. TKF
      1. Mission
      2. Vision

II. The Need
   A. The Community
   B. Family
   C. Individuals

III. Childhood Obesity
   A. Definition of overweight
   B. Definition of obese
   C. Epidemic
      1. Epidemiology
         a. Nationally
         b. Locally
      2. Etiology
   D. Growing up obese

IV. Approaching the challenge
   A. Public policy
   B. Community
   C. Organizational

D. Interpersonal
E. Individual

V. A strategic plan
   A. Health care
   B. School systems
   C. Child care and preschool providers
   D. Governmental Policies and Programs
   E. Businesses, work sites, and restaurants
   F. Community-based organizations and faith groups

VI. Objectives
   A. Foster and facilitate partnerships among community organizations and members
   B. Lower obesity rates in Lincoln children
   C. Obtain measurable improvements in nutrition and physical activity in Lincoln children
   D. Increase access to healthy foods and physical activity opportunities for all children and families
   E. Advocate for policy changes in support of these goals

VII. How you can help
   A. Join a working group
   B. Advocate
   C. Donate

VIII. Closing
   A. Community
   B. Family

In the example above, each point is marked by few words to help guide you through the opening, the body of the presentation, and the closing. This topic outline guides you, the writer, from connected topic to connected topic.

Topic outlines are useful to those who plan to give their presentations without writing them out completely. If you are an experienced presenter and feel that you have an exceedingly good handle on your topic, you might not need to go beyond the topic outline.

Sentence Outline Example:

Sentence outlines are a little more descriptive than the topic outline noted above. The advantage to the sentence outline is that you can make your presentation more active and descriptive. This will help you later as you move into the writing phase.

I. Begin by introducing yourself and the organization to the listeners.
    A. My name is Rick Helweg
        1. I am a student advocate for TKF
            a. Describe what student advocates do.
            b. Describe why I have been asked to speak to the listeners.
        2. Tell the listeners about my background and how I came to work with TKF.
    B. Tell the listeners what the mission of TKF is.
        1. The mission of TKF is to prevent and reduce childhood obesity by empowering Lincoln children and families to eat healthy and be active.
        2. TKF envisions creating community solutions for children's health.
II. Describe the need within the community for TKF.
    A. TKF is an organization dedicated to addressing the childhood obesity epidemic through utilization of the collaborative advantage.

B. TKF is the only organization in Lincoln that is committed to uniting organizations and community members to focus on a shared mission and commit to implementing measurable solutions that prevent and reduce childhood obesity among Lincoln children.

III. Give some background on the definition of childhood obesity.

A. Overweight and obesity are defined in children by the body mass index (BMI) measurement or the measure of weight adjusted for height using age and gender specific growth charts.

1. Overweight is defined as a BMI at or above the 85th percentile and lower than the 95th percentile for children of the same age and sex.

2. Obesity is defined as a BMI at or above the 95th percentile for children of the same age and sex.

B. As obesity rates have increased dramatically throughout the past 30 years in the United States in adults and children, obesity has become a national epidemic.

1. Epidemiology is the basic science of public health. It is a highly quantitative discipline based on principles of statistics and research methodologies.

a. Based on representative samples of U.S. children, nationally one-third of children are overweight or obese.

b. According to a recent report published by Trust for America's Health, Nebraska ranks as having the 21st highest percent of obese and overweight children in the United States, with 31.5 percent of Nebraska children measured as obese or overweight.

2. Etiology is the study of the causes of diseases and epidemics.

a. Obesity is the result of an imbalance of energy intake and energy expenditure.

b. Genetics, environment and behavior all contribute to obesity risk.

D. Describe the physical and social effects of growing up obese.

a. Obese children suffer from myriad of health consequences including but not limited to type II diabetes (formerly termed adult-onset diabetes), hypertension, early heart disease, sleep apnea, metabolic syndrome and early death.

b. Overweight and obese children are suffering from the psychosocial effects of this epidemic, often developing social phobias and depression, putting them at risk for increased school absenteeism rates, and hence, limiting their academic potential.

IV. Reversing the trend of obesity requires a comprehensive and coordinated approach that uses policy and environmental change to support and promote healthy lifestyles choices.

A. The public policy approach, ideally, addresses policy on a national, state, and local level.

B. The entire community should be engaged, and relationships among local organizations should be encouraged.

C. Social organizations and institutions should be engaged as a part of the community effort.

D. Interpersonal relationships from families, friends, and wider social networks are ways to organize and advocate for the cause.

E. The knowledge, attitudes, and skills of individuals are vital to the long-term goals of the organizational mission to prevent and reduce childhood obesity.

V. A strategic plan geared toward engaging the community in this effort must be made up of numerous working groups of individuals that represent a diverse cross section of the community.

    A. Health care providers are uniquely positioned as a voice of authority in their practice and as advocates in the community.

    B. Health is academic as there are numerous studies linking academic achievement with healthy eating and being physically active. The school systems working group will engage educators, students, parents, administrators, school board members, and after-school programs.

    C. Healthy behavior changes are sustained only if there are environmental policies that support these changes and the most effective way to do this is through governmental policies and programs.

    D. Community-based organizations and faith groups have connections to children and families, especially those disproportionately affected by the obesity epidemic, which can be used to increase healthy eating and physical activity opportunities.

    E. Youth are the strongest allies we have in this struggle as they are best suited to spreading the message in the schools, social organizations, and any place that their voice can be heard.

VI. TKF has met with community stakeholders to identify a realistic set of objectives directly related to the mission of the organization.

    A. TKF will foster and facilitate partnerships among community organizations and members.

VII. How can you help?

    A. You can help by joining a working group.

    B. You can help by advocating for healthy choices at your schools, churches, workplaces and community events.

    C. You can donate to help us carry out our mission.

VIII. Mobilizing and broadening (or widening) the net of working group members committed to promotion of the TKF mission are the next steps as we move forward with the strategic plan.

    A. TKF already has taken the important first steps toward engaging the Lincoln community as we have endeavored to design this strategic plan through the working group model.

    B. Families taking the first small steps in their homes is the most important part of the struggle to get a handle on this wide-ranging epidemic.

There is a difference in the information offered in this sentence outline as compared to the topic outline. Although the outlines are similar in the direction of the presentation, you can get a better feel for what information will be presented in the sentence outline.

If you feel the need to take small steps through the construction of your presentation, you might consider beginning your process by drafting a topic outline and following it with a sentence outline.

The sentence outline now offers you information and direction. Taking this outline to the next step of writing a first draft of a speech presentation is easier with this detailed road map.

As mentioned before, this might be all the drafting you will need to do for your speech. Indeed, you might choose to write your entire speech out, but do not expect to read directly from the speech and have it be compelling. Beginner speakers tend to use a speech draft as a lifeline — they start reading their speeches because they do not trust themselves to remember the points and hard-hitting turns of phrase they have worked so hard on in the drafting stage. However, no one will be interested in watching a speaker hunched over a sheet of paper, reading word-for-word and paying no attention to the audience. Perhaps a better method might be to outline your speech, have a good grasp on what you want to say in each point, and walk into your speech with your outline as a reference. Depending on the type of speech, you also could transfer your outline to note cards, which are not so noticeable.

You always can continue drafting your speech to make sure you covered all the information you intended to and are saying it in the best way possible. However, accept that you are not going to be able to give a successful speech by reading your final draft, and thus your speech might change slightly when you give it.

Some situations and types of speech might require a full speech to be written out. If you are giving a speech in a political situation or as a commencement speaker at a graduation, each word you say will have much more meaning than a presentation given on how to use a new piece of technology or an introduction speech of who Patrick Henry was. In these cases, your best bet will be to draft your speech fully. *Chapter 10 will give you tips on how to read your speech while still interacting with the audience.*

Drafting Your Speech

With a well-thought-out outline in front of you, preparing a draft of your presentation is not quite as hard a task as it might be without an outline. As a writer, you may fear staring blankly at a computer screen and not knowing what to write. With the sentence outline in front of you, this need never happen. Your outline always will be there to offer direction.

The first draft of your speech is a place where you can use your outline to draft a free-form text of what will eventually become your final speech. This means that you do not have to worry about anything except getting all your thoughts and information down in writing. You will have the opportunity to edit and clarify with later drafts. The first draft is all about filling out the blanks left in the outline and getting all your information gathered from your research out into one place.

As you write your first draft, stop every now and then to read what you have written aloud. After all, you are writing this presentation to be an oral presentation.

Be sure to give yourself plenty of time to write your first draft. You probably will discover that it is much easier to write a first draft than it will be to go back and properly edit and clean up your speech for presentation. Giving yourself adequate time to prepare your speech is vital, as you will require time to edit, practice and prepare any additional materials that will be needed to convey the message of your speech.

When the opening is written, you have a main body of a presentation prepared and a closing done then your first draft is complete. However, the first draft should not be your finished product. You might be happy with the work you have done, and the draft eventually might turn out to be close to what your finished product will be, but you still need to go over the text carefully to ensure everything in it is just as you would like it to be.

In examining your first draft, you need to consider a number of different factors:

- Does the draft follow the outline you prepared?
- Does the information you put forth align with your mission?
- Are the facts you deliver well researched and verifiable?
- Does the speech meet the needs of the audience?

Speaker's Point:

Do not edit your work as you write your first draft. Take the first draft opportunity to let your mind open up and let everything flow. If you have a solid outline, this should not be a difficult task. The problem with editing as you write is that you might tend to be too critical of your work, and you will begin to censor yourself. Hold off on the editing until after you have a complete first draft.

Editing Your Work

It is wise to set your first draft aside for at least 24 hours before you sit back down to edit and prepare your next draft. The time that the draft is set aside will allow you to clear your mind, so you can return to your work with a fresh perspective.

Editing is the process of reviewing the work you have done. Editing the draft is the process of carefully going through the work to check for errors, continuity issues, missed ideas and flow.

When you return to your speech to start the editing process, read what you have in a different medium. If you wrote your speech on a computer, print it out and read the printout. If you wrote your speech by hand, type it up and read it. Reading the work in a different format is a good way to see the work in a different light.

Before you start to strike things out of the document or add anything, read the work several times. As you are writing a speech, do not forget to read it aloud. It is helpful as you read aloud to record what you have read. Listen to the recording. As you listen to the recording, take notes on what you have written. There is no need to note your vocal presentation or how your voice sounds. Your notes at this point should focus on the words, the flow and the continuity of the text of your speech.

After you have read the text to yourself and aloud and after your have listened to the recording, you can sit down at your chosen medium and start to edit.

If you created your first draft on a computer, save the draft as a new file, so you can edit the work while keeping the first draft in its first form. Lay the two files down on the desktop and start to go through your first draft making notes as you go.

Note your initial feelings as to the length, content and flow. If you feel that anything is missing, make a note of that. If you think you would like to add anything to better illustrate specific points, make note of that.

The following example has been put together to show the differences between a first and a second draft of a presentation prepared for TKF. The main text of the presentation shows the second draft of the speech. In the margin, you will note the text that has been edited away from the first draft of the speech. Note that quite a bit of text has been removed from the initial draft of the presentation. In editing the speech, the writer was able clarify and make the presentation shorter by removing information that the audience could research at home.

Note the references to slide possibilities in the notes in the margin of the text. As the speech goes into a possible third draft or if it is reformulated to a fuller outline for the speaker, a guide to a slide or PowerPoint presentation will be a part of the final draft.

To follow is an example of the editing process. First off, we'll start by writing and editing the introduction. This is the place to introduce yourself as well as the topic you will be covering. Note the changes made throughout the editing process.

▶ **The overall impressions of the first draft are that the text was far too long, and a good deal of information, while vital to the organization, is not necessary for the intended audience.**

It would help if a personal story were added to the text. The story of a child or family affected by the issue.

"Good evening. My name is Rick Helweg, and I'm a student advocate for TKF. First, I'd like to thank you for offering us the opportunity to visit with you this evening to let you know a little about TKF. We also would like to talk a little about what we can do together to make our community a healthier place to live.

▶ **The presenter might start by introducing themselves and relating how and/or why they are dedicating themselves to the organization and its mission. The opening of the presentation is simple and straightforward. The mission and vision of the organization is well thought out and quite clear. This opening tells the listener exactly who the organization is, what it does and what its vision is.**

I came to TKF two years ago as a student looking to volunteer my time to a worthy cause. I have many friends who are affected by obesity every day. I am an active advocate for physical activity and healthy foods. The mission of TKF is close to my heart.

The mission of TKF is to prevent and reduce childhood obesity by empowering Lincoln children and families to eat healthy and be active. TKF envisions creating community solutions for children's health.

TKF is the only organization in Lincoln that is committed to uniting organizations and community members to focus on a shared mission and commit to implementing measurable solutions that prevent and reduce childhood obesity among Lincoln children.

After the speaker clearly introduces the topic, the body of the speech comes next. This is where all of the supporting points are made. Here is an example of the beginning of the editing process with a body. Take note of the critical cuts and helpful notes that the author inserts into the paper. Though this is only part of the speech, the rest of the speech should follow a similar format.

The childhood obesity epidemic has reached alarming levels. It is an epidemic affecting not only the physical health of children, families, and community, but also their psychosocial, academic, and economic potential. Multiple studies show increasing levels over the last 30 years, with a tripling of prevalence over that time period. Obese children face myriad of health, emotional, and social consequences as a result of this epidemic. At least one-third of Lincoln's children are considered overweight or obese. Minority children, impoverished children, and children who live in certain Lincoln neighborhoods without access to healthy foods and safe play spaces are disproportionately affected by the obesity epidemic. These populations have even higher rates of obesity, diabetes, early heart disease and are at risk for shorter life expectancies.

TKF is a 501(c)(3) non-profit organization founded in 2008 by Karla Lester, M.D., who left her practice to address the growing epidemic of poor nutrition and physical inactivity in our community's children. Working in partnership with community members, TKF envisions creating a community solution to this growing epidemic.

Overweight and obesity is defined in children by the body mass index (BMI) measurement, or the measure of weight adjusted for height using age and gender specific growth charts.

BMI is defined as weight divided by the square of height. BMI levels correlate with body fat and also correlate with concurrent health risks, especially cardiovascular risk factors. For children, the distribution of BMI changes with age.

As a result, percentiles specific for age and gender define under-weight, healthy weight, overweight, and obesity in children. Obesity risk is also determined by screening family history, assessing physical activity and nutrition behaviors, a review of systems and physical examination for comorbidities, which taken altogether determine the need for intervention.

▶ **Some good illustrations can be used to make the points covered here clearer. PowerPoint slides illustrating BMI and the growth of the epidemic nationally and locally will help illustrate.**

As obesity rates have increased dramatically over the last 30 years in the U.S. in both adults and children, obesity has become a national epidemic. Data from the CDC from 2003-2004 and 2005-2006 indicated that two-thirds of U.S. adults were either obese or overweight. Based on representative samples of U.S. children, nationally one-third of children are overweight or obese. According to the esteemed Robert Wood Johnson Foundation, we are raising the first generation of youth who will live sicker and shorter lives than their parents. The childhood obesity epidemic has become a public health emergency with tripling of prevalence rates since 1980. According to a recent report published by Trust for America's Health, Nebraska ranks as having the 21st highest percent of obese and overweight children in the U.S., with 31.5 percent of Nebraska children measured as obese or overweight. The childhood obesity epidemic disproportionately affects children who are minority, live in poverty, and/or live in neighborhoods without access to healthy foods and safe play spaces. These disparities are demonstrated nationally and in our community.

The economic burden of the obesity epidemic on our community is high. Rising health care costs, decreased workforce productivity, increased school absenteeism rates have an economic effect on all of our citizens.

Obese children suffer from myriad of health consequences including but not limited to type II diabetes (formerly termed adult-onset diabetes), hypertension, early heart disease, sleep apnea, metabolic syndrome, and early death. Overweight and obese children are suffering from the psychosocial effects of this epidemic in great numbers, often developing social phobias and depression, putting them at risk for increased school absenteeism rates and hence limiting their academic potential.

► **A good place for a personal story**

As we go about our work, we have the opportunity to meet with many in the community that are personally affected by this epidemic. We know that many of you are, as well. We received an email recently from a school nurse wanting to be become more involved with our organization as she struggled with how to deal with a 9-year-old girl that weighed 200 pounds. The child, a third grader, was falling asleep in class, unable to concentrate on her work, unable to fully partake in recess and PE class, and may be suffering a whole host of health issues related to her weight. The nurse's attempts to communicate with the girl's family over the issue are met with some amount of indifference and excuses that are, to some extent, issues that we, as a community must deal with such as safe places to play, access to affordable healthy food, and affordable programs that will help this young girl and her family.

Obesity is the result of an imbalance of energy intake and energy expenditure. Genetics, environment, and behavior all contribute to obesity risk. The rapid increase in prevalence of children who are obese and overweight cannot be explained by genetics only. Changes in nutrition and physical activity behaviors and environments that do not support healthy choices have caused this public health problem to move to epidemic proportions, with disparate affect on populations.

▶ **The following text was cut from the first draft of this speech:**

The Planning Process

TKF has worked on the creation of a three-tiered strategic plan that will allow it to effectively carry out its mission. The three tiers of this plan are a business plan, a development plan and a program plan.

The development plan will develop mechanisms to raise needed funds through foundation and corporate grants, develop a plan to raise funds through individual donations, design a system of corporate sponsorships, and design a program of planned giving that will help to provide long-term support for the organization. The development plan will also leverage TKF's extensive community of partners to assist in raising the resources necessary to carry out its mission.

Perhaps the most important part of this three-tiered plan is the program plan.

TKF is engaged in creating community solutions to the epidemic of childhood obesity. The first step in this process was to hold a series of round-table discussions with the community-at-large to address the issue of the epidemic of childhood obesity. These forums defined the precise nature of the epidemic; examined the history; defined the current state of the community; and explored potential community solutions.

For planning purposes, the community-at-large was identified as six distinct working groups:
- *Health care*
- *School systems*
- *Governmental policies and programs*
- *Community-based organizations and faith groups*

After a community-wide summit and the series of working group forums had occurred, TKF staff and board examined the information gathered and prioritized it, creating a Call to Action with measurable objectives.

TKF intends to continue its activities that address the childhood obesity epidemic by growing partnerships that crosscut all sectors of the community and by implementing a long-term strategic plan that has been created as a result of working group input, community input, and other such initiatives from across the country. TKF then will work as an organizational board to determine phases and priorities of implementation and seek further funding. TKF will advocate for policy changes in support of their goals.

Working to meet children and families where they live, learn, work, and play is the recommendation of the RWJF and the CDC. Our collaborative initiative stands to serve thousands of infants, toddlers, school-aged children, and adolescents in the Lincoln community. For instance, working as a community based organization with the Lincoln Public Schools, there is the potential to foster the development of policies and strategies which will help prevent the development of obesity in thousands of Lincoln children and also prevent the development of diseases, such as early heart disease and type II diabetes, which are caused by obesity.

> *The final step is to edit your conclusion. The following is an example of a conclusion that has been worked through and rethought. Make sure all of your main points are covered and your ending is clear.*

Evaluation: How can we measure our success?
1. *Measure BMI and fitness levels in LPS students and develop a method to measure BMI in early childhood.*
2. *Track eating and physical activity behaviors of children.*
3. *Ensure that a formal public health evaluation component is incorporated into the design of all projects and programs.*
4. *A developed best-practice guide implemented to evaluate our multi-level collaborative model.*

Mobilizing and broadening (or widening) the net of working group members committed to promotion of the TKF mission are the next steps as we move forward with the battle against this epidemic.

The sustainability of tour actions will come with the committed partnerships being forged as we engage in finding this community solution to the epidemic of childhood obesity. To make systemic changes leading to healthy behavior changes in our community, will require engagement and collaboration of key stakeholders, organizational, and individual partners. You can be a partner in this struggle that is so vital to the health of our children and our community. You can help by joining a working group. You can help by advocating for healthy choices at your schools, churches, workplaces, and community events. You can donate to help us carry out our mission.

▶ **The closing of the first draft has been changed to insert a greater call to action. The following was the closing of the first draft:**

TKF has already taken the important first steps toward engaging the greater Lincoln community as we have endeavored to design this strategic plan through the working group model. As we grow and engage these working groups and implement these long-term plans we expect that our mission and vision will become sustainable and we will achieve our set goals.

You can be a partner in this struggle that is so vital to the health of our children and our community. You can help by joining a working group. You can help by advocating for healthy choices at your schools, churches, workplaces, and community events. You can donate to help us carry out our mission.

Go to our website: teachakidtofish.org to find out more. Let's work together to make our community the healthiest community it can be. Thank you!

The second draft

The edited draft offered as an example above can now be considered as the second draft of the TKF speech. If you were to compare the second draft to the first draft, you would note several differences:

- The second draft is about 45 percent shorter than the first draft.

- The second draft tells a more personal story.

- The second draft made room for media illustration of facts.

- The second draft makes a clearer call to action and informs the listener where they can find more information.

Each of the points made above comparing the second draft to the first draft make the second draft a more effective presentation. As you edit and hone your presentation and take the presentation from outline to first draft and then on to second draft, you should become more conscious of your audience.

The second draft of the TKF presentation will run about 20 minutes. The first draft, delivered as it was written, would have probably taken about 35 minutes to deliver. The general rule is that a speech will read as long as your initial aloud reading if you read at a normal speaking rate. After you complete your second draft, just give it a timed reading aloud, and you will have a good idea of how long it will be. However, this might not be the time it will take you to give the speech on the big day. People tend to speak much faster when they are nervous. *Chapter 10 will give some tips on being conscious of your speed and slowing yourself down while giving your speech.*

The first draft of the presentation was filled with many facts and bullet points that, while important to the organization, might not have been as vital for the listener. Instead, in the second draft, the speaker informed the listener where they could find that information if they were interested in doing so.

The second draft offered a story as example of a young student and an elementary school nurse that is concerned about the health of the student. The story is a good way of grounding the need for action concerning the epidemic of childhood obesity.

The second draft notes specific places where slides or Power-Point illustrations might help to make the growth of the epidemic easier to see. *Chapter 6 will examine these tools a little more closely.*

The second draft includes a clearer call to action than the first draft. For an organization such as TKF, this call to action is of the utmost importance.

Take Your Speech for a Test Drive

Now that you are comfortable with the draft of your speech, you can take it for a test drive. If you read your first draft aloud to yourself and were able to record it as your read, that first recording will serve you well as you compare it to the recording of your second draft.

Read your speech aloud. Read your speech aloud several times, keeping track of the time it takes to read from beginning to end. Each time you read, you will become more comfortable with the pacing of the speech and the flow of ideas.

After you have read the speech aloud several times, make another recording of yourself reading through your second draft. After you have recorded yourself, listen to your recording and take note of your pace, your vocal quality, and the flow of ideas from beginning to end.

When you initially recorded your first draft, you were interested primarily in the text of your speech. Now, as you record and listen to your second draft, you will start to focus on your delivery as well.

Listening to your second draft, continue to consider comprehensibility of mission and vision, but also begin to make note of your vocal quality. You know now, however, if you can or cannot be heard. You will hear on the tape if you are garbling words, speaking too fast or cutting off the beginnings or ending of certain words. For anything that you hear on your recording that you feel you will need to work on to be heard and/or understood, make note of it.

A Third Draft?

After you have read, re-read, recorded, and listened to your speech several times, you can make the decision as to whether you think a third draft is necessary. You might ask yourself the following questions:

- Does the speech accomplish what I want to accomplish?

- Does the speech deliver the information I have been asked to deliver?

- Does the speech fit within the time suggested?

If you are comfortable with the answers to these questions, you probably do not need to go through a third draft. You will, however, probably continue to edit the speech until the day you present it. Each time you deliver a speech in rehearsal or to an audience, you probably will make note of things that worked and things that did not work particularly well. In the speech being prepared by TKF, statistics will change and, as such, changes will be made to the presentation. With each element that is added to the presentation, changes will be made. Slides, audience, audience size, and facilities all will have an effect on your presentation.

A live presentation is a living thing with many variables to contend with each time you deliver it. As such, nothing can be written in stone. Your second draft might be the draft of the speech you are comfortable moving forward with, but it will change. It will never be the same two times in a row.

To Memorize or Not?

Each time you read your speech in the editing process and listen to your speech after having recorded it, you will become more familiar with the flow of information. The idea of standing in front of a large group of strangers to speak is rather daunting to many people. *The topic of stage fright is discussed in Chapter 8.* The question asked above, "To memorize or not?" will depend on your comfort with the subject, the speech itself and the audience.

It is a bad idea to prepare a presentation and stand before your audience to read verbatim from your prepared text. You have seen these speakers before. What they lack is a connection to their audience. It is nearly impossible to create a connection with your audience if your eyes are glued to your text. Likewise, it is not recommended that you memorize your speech word-for-word. The reason for this is that it is too easy to get stuck when you forget a line or a paragraph, transpose ideas, and fall into a repetitive pattern that will leave your audience feeling numbed with boredom. Audiences can tell when a speaker is repeating a memorized speech, and it can come off stiff and lacking passion.

The answer to this question depends on your comfort level. Only you can determine which is the best solution for you. If you are comfortable with the material but not comfortable speaking in front of an audience, you might choose a sentence outline that is easy to follow. If you are uncomfortable with the material, you might choose to speak with a fully realized text to follow:

- You can choose to take the speaker's podium armed with the entire text of your speech, carefully prepared to allow you to refer to it when you need to but, at the same time, maintaining contact with your audience.

- You can choose to take the speaker's podium with your sentence outline that will guide you from point to point armed with the statements that direct your presentation.

- You can deliver your presentation guided only by your topic outline or note cards if you are completely comfortable with your topic and before an audience.

After you have spoken on your topic numerous times, you will probably feel comfortable standing and speaking to audiences without the aid of an outline. To start with, however, it is wise to be armed with notes of some kind.

Of course, the type of presentation also can influence what notes you have going into the speech. If you will have a podium or table in front of you to hide notes or your speech draft easily, these notes will come in handy. Even in a debate, you usually can keep notes in front of you. However, if you are giving a demonstration of a new type of technology with the new machine itself, it might not be practical to have your notes in front of your nose at all times. For impromptu speeches, or at least speeches that should seem impromptu such as an acceptance speech or a toast at a wedding, pulling out a huge handful of notes or several pages of a drafted speech can detract from the message you intend to convey to your audience. Consider all these situations when you are deciding whether to memorize your speech, memorize just the main points of your speech, take your full speech in with you or only take notes in with you.

Nontraditional Presentation Methods

All the examples noted so far in this chapter and the exampled outlines in the previous chapter refer to speech presentations that are of a traditional nature: in other words, speech presentations in which the speaker stands before an audience and delivers a message and is, perhaps, aided by a slide or PowerPoint presentation.

Depending on the nature of your presentation, you might be inclined to take another path. If you are giving a presentation about the merits of opera, you might do well to sing your presentation. If your speech is about American poetry of the 19th century, you might consider writing your speech in verse.

Many types of presentations will not allow you the luxury of preparing a presentation ahead of time. Presentations that call for question and answer, debates and impromptu presentations will give you little time to formulate a presentation/response. These types of presentations take the ability and skill of listening, the tools of a pen and paper and practice.

Debates and Q&As

Just because you cannot write up an outline to prepare yourself for your presentation does not mean you cannot bring notes with you. For many types of question and answer periods or debates, you will have a podium or table to set notes on, and the audience does not mind if you refer back to those notes. If you anticipate being involved in a formal debate or question and answer period, take some time to research your topic thoroughly. You will want to know the material backward and forward. You also might want to create a note page that has some of the hard-hitting facts and statistics you found that support your topic so you do not have to memorize lots of figures or dates.

For question and answer situations, try to think of any questions or concerns you found when doing your research on the topic. You also can ask friends and family what questions they would have on your topic. Once you have these questions, you can make sure you know the answer or at least have facts that answer the question written down on the notes you will take with you to the presentation.

A debate is a good example of when to know the other side of the argument as well as you know your own side. If you anticipate your opponent's arguments and points, you can find research and arguments to refute each of them. You even can set up your notes paper by opposing arguments. Then as your opponent makes each one, you will have all the information you need to refute him or her right in front of you.

Finally, do not underestimate the importance of listening. Listening is a skill. A skill is developed through practice. You can practice the skill by working with a partner to ask you specific questions related to the topic on which you will be speaking. As the question is being asked, practice listening and noting pertinent thoughts as the question is being asked. This is also a skill to have if or when you are involved in a debate. Listen, note your response, and use the note to organize your response. Even if you are thoroughly familiar with a specific subject matter, being able to listen and offer an organized response to a question is a skill that requires practice.

Nontraditional example

We can return to the earlier example in which Patrick Henry has been invited to speak to a group of school students, and you have been asked to introduce him. Your goal has been stated in the supposition above: to introduce. You also must consider the fact that Mr. Henry is an invited guest and should be welcomed.

If you were to consider taking this introductory presentation down an original and creative pathway, you might consider a number of options:

- You could start by dressing in period costume and assuming the character of one that knew or was a contemporary of Patrick Henry.

- Research what biographers and contemporaries of Henry's wrote about him.

- Choose to address the audience as an ally or opponent of Patrick Henry's.

- Model your introduction of Patrick Henry as if delivered by your chosen contemporary.

Example of a nontraditional presentation:

To introduce Patrick Henry to a group of elementary school students, you might choose to assume the character of Edward Carrington. Research has informed you that Edward Carrington was a young delegate in the colony of Virginia in March of 1775 when Patrick Henry delivered his famous "Give me liberty, or give me death" speech.

Research can provide the speaker with nearly all the information needed to inform him or her why Patrick Henry is a figure that stands out in American history. The words of his contemporaries would do well to inform the audience of young listeners who it is they were about to meet.

Remember that the presenter in this case has three simple goals:

- Welcome Patrick Henry.
- Thank Patrick Henry.
- Give the students a little background on Patrick Henry.

The order described above is not necessarily the order in which the described tasks need to be presented. They are just a checklist of what needs to happen as the speaker prepares his or her presentation. This checklist, though, in the same order or in a different order, serves well as a topic outline for this short and simple, though nontraditional, presentation.

As noted earlier, the most difficult thing about making a presentation is keeping it simple. If you were to choose to make this introductory presentation in the character of Edward Carrington, it is vital that you remember the two points noted in Chapter 3:

- The audience is a group of students.
- The presenter of the introduction is not the featured speaker.

The topic outline of this non-traditional introductory presentation might look something like this:

I. Edward Carrington introduction
      A. Who I am
      B. Why I am here

II. Who Patrick Henry is
      A. Abbreviated biography
      B. Why we remember Patrick Henry

III. Thank Patrick Henry for joining us

IV. Welcome Patrick Henry

The basic topic outline for this introduction should suffice to write an introduction that should run two to four minutes at the longest. Remember, this speech is more about the guest.

"Young ladies and young gentlemen, please allow me to introduce myself. My name is Edward Carrington, and I was a young resident of the American colony of Virginia in March 1775. On March 23, 1775, I was invited to St. John's Church in Richmond, Virginia, to hear a discussion about the future of our young colonies of America. One of the speakers in this discussion is our guest here today. That man is Patrick Henry. When I heard Mr. Henry speak about his feelings for his home, his beloved Virginia and America I declared, "Let me be buried on this spot!" for I then believed that I would never hear anything so beautiful and faithful again.

Patrick Henry is, indeed, a Founding Father of these United States of America. Patrick Henry is one of the most memorable leaders of the American revolutionary struggle against the rule of the British Crown, a colonel of the First Virginia Regiment, a governor of Virginia and an American hero.

We would like to thank Mr. Patrick Henry for joining us today to talk to us about American patriotism. So, without further adieu, please welcome Mr. Patrick Henry."

This example runs about a minute and a half. The example, a first draft of an introductory speech, accomplishes what it set out to accomplish and does so in a clear and concise manner.

This nontraditional presentation is just an example of an infinite variety of speech presentations that an individual might be asked to give. Whether you are to give an acceptance speech, an informative presentation, or are involved in a persuasive debate, many creative avenues are open to you to make your presentation memorable. If the situation will allow, take your time to consider offering your audience something that will be completely different from anything they have seen or experienced before.

Many situations are best served by more traditional presentation methods, but if you think there is an opportunity to be creative, by all means, make your presentation memorable.

Writing Wrap-Up

Knowing how to gather facts into clear lines of thought, outline, and write an effective presentation is a skill that takes practice. Many writers will tell you that to be an effective communicator, whether you are writing, speaking or playing a musical instrument, you have to practice every day. Methods of practice, as it relates to public speaking, will be explored in Chapter 8. To practice your writing, make a point of writing on a daily basis. Many people write every day and do not even think about it. Whether you write for school, write emails, social media posts or daily journals, you can think about any of these as daily practice.

Be mindful of your writing as you strive for clarity and conciseness. On the other hand, learn how to and practice stream-of-conscious writing. Choose a subject and just start writing about it. Write out everything you might know or feel about it. Go back to the first draft of the TKF presentation and note how much information was written out. This was not done in a stream-of-conscious manner as it followed an outline, but it is a text in which the writer dumped everything out onto the page and then used the editing process to make the piece more clear and concise.

When you sit down to write, write. Do not allow the blank page to stare back and defeat you. If you have been asked to deliver a presentation on a specific subject, whether that subject is childhood obesity, Patrick Henry, or the toast at your uncle Bernie's wedding, note the subject, the occasion, the reason you have been asked to speak, the audience, and then let your mind open up to all the possibilities.

You have been asked to deliver the speech for a reason. Embrace the opportunity and show them what you have.

CASE STUDY: TODD FITZGERALD

Todd Fitzgerald
Lincoln, Nebraska

Todd Fitzgerald is an active community volunteer in Lincoln, Nebraska.

My journey into public speaking started when I was in the eighth grade. I got duped into joining the speech team at my junior high school. I always loved talking, and I saw this as a way I could talk as much as I wanted, not realizing I would be participating in speech tournaments. My first speech tourney was at St. Cecilia School in Omaha. As we prepared, I realized that I like the impromptu speeches (which looking back were tough). I got my topic, planned out my speech, and when it was my time to present, I was nervous at first, but I realized when I started speaking, I believed in my topic. My confidence grew as the speech went along, and the judges were captivated by what I was saying. After that, I always would look for opportunities to speak, readings at church, and volunteering for presentations anyway I could. My speeches are more informational/motivational with a splash of entertainment. I think that the elements of an effective speech are:

- A strong belief and passion about your topic
- Being able to create a compelling story
- Identify why you believe in what you are speaking about.
- Create a story to which your audience can relate.

A mentor of mine once said, "Facts sell, stories tell." If you believe in the topic you are presenting, your audience will be able to feel your passion and energy and will buy in to what you are saying. I believe that engaging your audience starts before your speech or presentation begins. Greeting people, if you get a chance, as they walk in helps you get a feel for your audience. Creating a strong opening will capture your audience's attention and build their interest, but you have to make sure you keep them engaged. You are going to lose some who might not be interested in what you have to say, but it is vital that you stay positive and focused because there is a chance you might say something that brings them back on board to what you are speaking about. I believe it is all about the first impression. You have one chance to make an impression on your audience. I think the best tip would be to research and become an expert on the topic or the organization you are speaking about. Being familiar with your topic and prepared will build your confidence. Another tip would be work to build a connection with your audience. If you have done research and properly prepared your confidence, belief and passion will be able to be recognized and appreciated by the audience. Be yourself. Do not try to be something or someone you are not. The audience will be able to tell. You have to be genuine, empathetic, and true, and the audience will appreciate it. Inexperienced speakers make several common mistakes. One would be not being prepared. Another common mistake is not having an understanding of the topic or organization to which they are speaking. Not being yourself also is a common mistake. If you are trying to be something you are not, the audience will be able to tell if you are being genuine or fake.

As a speaker, I place importance on listening because it allows me to be a more productive and effective speaker. When you are in a room before you speak, listening to the people talk, their conversations give you insight as to the mood and the type of audience you will have. When I was younger and just getting into public speaking, I was always afraid I would forget what I was presenting or that people would make fun of me. I would take a deep breath, close my eyes, and pray. It would be a short prayer, but I would pray for the courage to be the best that I could be and that everything was going to be all right. Being prepared is the best way to ameliorate the fear of public speaking. Give yourself enough time to go over your speech, but do not spend too much time — maybe ten to 20 minutes — before you present. Work the room. Take time to meet and greet people as they come into the room. Building a rapport with the audience, you will find someone who you either know or with whom you connect. That person has now become your biggest fan and supporter and not even realized it. Find him or her in the crowd, and when you give your speech, give it as if you are having a conversation with that person. It will help decrease some of your fear and tension. Relax and meditate. Find a nice quite area, close your eyes, and breathe slow, deep breaths. This will help you find that happy place we all like to go in times of stress. There are so many effective public speakers that I can think of, but individuals like John Maxwell, Vince Lombardi, Coach Mike Kryzewski, and the late Jim Rohn come to mind. Anyone who can captivate an audience, generate excitement, create energy, and change the feelings of the people who are listening qualifies as effective. The individuals listed above have or had a unique ability to change the feeling and emotions of their perspective audiences. They are able to build relationships with the audience with the use of their words, create energy, and map out a vision for the people who are listening.

Weak public speakers are those who are not prepared or have not done any research on what they are presenting. If you are not prepared, then the material you present will not be effective, and you will lose the interest of the audience. The audience will know you are not prepared. Be yourself. Understand your strengths and weaknesses, and tailor your speech around your strengths. Be prepared and take time to put thought into your speech or presentation. If you are presenting to an organization, and they give you a topic, make sure the material you have in your speech is tailored to their specific vision, mission, or beliefs. Take time to meet and greet. Get there early so you can move about the room and introduce yourself so the audience is familiar with you in a more relaxed and natural setting. Practice ten to 20 minutes before you present. Go over your speech. By this time, you will have gone over it and practiced it hundreds of times. The ten to 20 minutes before will just solidify your confidence. Take time to relax and meditate. Find a quiet place to go, close your eyes, visualize giving the speech, and breathe. When the time comes to present, get on the stage, and be confident. Believe and be the best you can be.

Chapter 6

Auxiliary Tools

A s you have gone through the process of writing your outline and then drafting your speech presentation, you might have considered a variety of ways in which you might strengthen your ability to tell your story. In the drafted outline examples in the previous chapter of the presentation for Teach a Kid to Fish, there were several references to slides or PowerPoint slides to help make a point, display the organizational logo or reinforce a particular point-of-view.

A PowerPoint presentation or a slide show are just two auxiliary tools at your disposal when it comes to increasing the dynamic nature of your presentation. The reasons presenters choose to employ these auxiliary tools are as diverse as the tools available. You might use these tools to reinforce a specific point. You could choose to employ auxiliary tools to define points in a sidebar manner. Graphic charts can be displayed to show trends more clearly. Props can be a visual symbol of recognition for your audience. Films can be used to tell the stories that might be better told by people who could not be present at your event. Music and sound can be employed to enhance the feeling and flow of a presentation. The list of tools and how and why to use them are endless and are only limited by your own needs and creativity.

There are a number of important points to consider when you make the decision to use any of the auxiliary tools available to you:

- Does the use of an auxiliary tool enhance the presentation?

- Do you have the know-how to employ the auxiliary tool properly?

- Do you have the technology necessary to use the tool properly?

- Can the venue in which you are speaking support your use of the tool?

If you choose to use an auxiliary tool in presentation, treat your preparation of this added dimension in the same way that you prepared your speech. Draft your use of the tool. Edit your use of the tool. Although a tool such as a PowerPoint presentation can make your speech more dynamic, it also can take away from the message you might be trying to convey in numerous ways.

If your use of the tool is not smooth, you might find yourself getting caught up in trying to make the technology work. The frustration this can cause will take away from what you are there to do.

If you plan to use an auxiliary tool, also make sure your presentation will be fine without the tool. Technology has a way of not working at the most inopportune moments.

If you plan to bring your own equipment, make sure you have a place to draw power from (if necessary) and that you can operate the technology with little or no assistance.

The bottom-line of working with any auxiliary tools in your presentation is that you have to be ready for any possible problems. The key to using any of the auxiliary tools covered in this chapter is being able to carry off your presentation without the tools. In other words, the tools should be there to help you do your job but you cannot count on the tools to do your job for you.

The short list of auxiliary tools available to you includes:

- Slide show/PowerPoint
- Print
- Video
- Sound
- Body language
- Outside the box

Slide show/PowerPoint

A PowerPoint presentation has, for the most part, taken the place of the slide presentation as the go-to auxiliary tool used to support speech presentations. A simple example of a short slide presentation that the speaker presenting the Teach a Kid to Fish presentation might offer could look something like this:

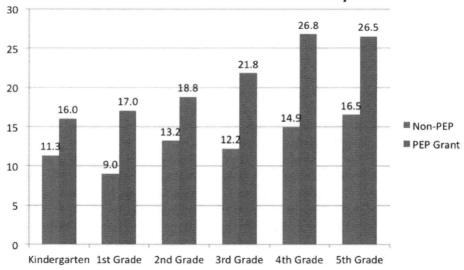

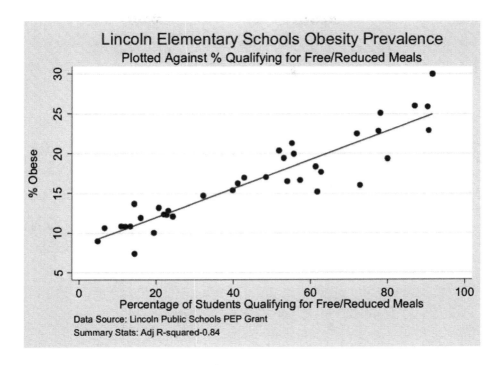

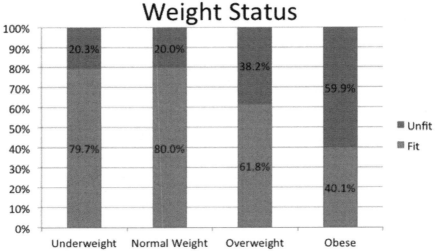

The slides include an organizational logo highlighting that this organization works to prevent childhood obesity. This logo can be displayed from the opening of the presentation and can remain on display after the other slides have been shown.

A slide presentation such as the one above can be a powerful tool to help you increase the dynamics of your presentation. A slide presentation also can be a dangerous crutch if not employed properly.

A lengthy slide presentation might have a negative effect on your audience. Consider the fact that you might have to dim some lighting for the slides to be seen. An extended time in the dark (especially if your presentation is given after a meal) might cause some in your audience to fall asleep.

Do not fall into the trap of reading your slides word for word. Remember that you should use slides only to support what you have written. You usually can assume your audience knows how to read. You can speak about what the slide shows and explain anything on the slide that needs to be explained, but avoid reading the slide text word for word.

Example: In the Teach a Kid to Fish slides shown earlier, the second bar graph refers to PEP grant schools. The presenter might have to explain that PEP grant schools are schools participating in a specially funded fitness, physical education, and activity program. The presenter also can speak to the specific meanings of each of the slides. However, if the following slide were to be included:

Cynthia M. White PEP Grant

- ~$500, 000 three year grant to improve the fitness, physical education skills, and activity levels of students in 17 LPS elementary schools
- Includes tracking of weight status in all 37 elementary schools (comparison of grant schools to non grant schools)
- Includes tracking of fitness levels in 4th and 5th graders in all 37 LPS elementary schools.

The presenter might just allow the audience to read the information while setting the stage for the accompanying data to follow. It would be a mistake for the presenter to read the slide word for word.

Decide what it is you want to achieve with your slides and allow them to help you in your presentation. Like the writing, you do not want to burden your audience with too much information, especially if it does not pertain to your presentation. If slides can help your presentation, use them. If slides are only there to make your presentation look cool or because you do not have much to say, think twice about what you are doing.

Questions to ask when considering a slide show/PowerPoint presentation:

- What equipment is available where the presentation will be done?

- What equipment will you need to provide?

- Who will run the slides/PowerPoint?

- Can the technology be prepared and tested in advance?

- What will you do if the technology does not operate as planned?

Print

You might consider using printed material to assist you in your presentation. Printed material works in much the same way as slides do, but it does have a major advantage: Printed material allows your audience to read at their leisure, and the audience can take it with them when they leave.

The speaker offering the Teach a Kid to Fish presentation probably would not consider offering the bar graph slides as printed material but might present the audience with a selection of printed matter that could include:

- A recent organizational annual report

- A recent organizational newsletter

- Information on how an individual might become involved with the organization as a volunteer

- Information on how an individual might donate money to the organization

It is not always necessary to refer to the printed material you offer an audience, especially if the material speaks for itself. In the case of the suggested printed material above, the Teach a Kid to Fish speaker could refer to the material in the closing of the speech call-to-action if, indeed, material referring to volunteerism or donations were to be present.

Like a slide show, printed material should be offered as supplemental information. Do not rely on the printed material to do your job of delivering the message.

Questions to ask when considering using printed material as an auxiliary tool:

- How many copies of each piece will be required to ensure everyone in attendance gets a copy?

- Should you provide additional copies?

- How will the material be distributed?

- Should you/do you need to provide materials in more than one language?

Video

The use of video also can be a powerful supplemental tool in delivering your message. With the digital capabilities available to nearly everyone with a computer today, video can be prepared and used much more easily than at anytime in the past. Video can be projected the same way you project a slide show. Video can be used along with the slide show you prepare and even can be inserted into the slide show in many programs.

Video, like a slide show or printed matter, is limited only by the needs and creativity of the presenter. Computer programs can animate data to make it come alive, cell phones can be used to record interviews with individuals pertinent to the subject of your presentation, and YouTube® videos can be a great, captivating tool.

The strengths and dangers of video are the same as they are for slide presentations. You must remember to use only what is necessary to the subject of your presentation. *You* have been asked to give the presentation, not some video presence you found on YouTube.

The presenter of the Teach a Kid to Fish presentation might choose to use video in the following manner:

- To present a short local news report on the increase of overweight/obese children in local schools

- To present animated graphic data showing the increase in overweight/obese children in local schools

- To present a video statement in support of the organization offered by the mayor or the superintendent of schools

Try to avoid offering the bulk of your presentation on video. Often, a message you plan to deliver on a video screen is more effective when delivered by you, the presenter. The length of the video you choose should be determined by the message the video delivers. That said, you should try to keep video clips to under a minute or two. Think of it this way: You are preparing and delivering a live presentation. Inserting a video into the presentation will alter the tone and flow of your presentation. Video is a very powerful tool that should be used with great thought and care. If you choose to employ a video clip, keep it short, and make sure that it directly relates to and enhances your message.

If you choose to employ video technology, make sure you have the proper equipment that matches the size of the venue. Do not show a large group of people a video on your small laptop screen. Likewise, an overly large screen in a small space can be overwhelming.

If you plan to show a video, be prepared to come equipped with your own equipment if you cannot do a technical run-through the day of your presentation. Even if you are able to do a technical run-through, be sure you arrive with your own laptop.

Beware of the effect of video. Like slide shows, you may have to dim the lights of a room to allow for decent viewing. If you have an overly lengthy video that you plan to show at a time of the day when your audience might be a bit tired, you will run the risk of hearing a few snores.

Questions to ask when considering a video presentation:

- What equipment is available where the presentation will be done?
- What equipment will you need to provide?
- Will the lights in the venue need to be lowered for the audience to see the video?
- Who will run the video?
- Who will lower and raise the lights if necessary?
- Can the technology be prepared and tested in advance?
- What will you do if the technology does not operate as planned?

Sound

Sound is an auxiliary tool that might not be as widely used as PowerPoint or video, but it can be just as powerful. When you first think of sound, you might consider music in your presentation, but depending on what your presentation is, you also might consider an endless list of sounds that can enhance your presentation.

Depending on the venue and setting in which your presentation will be done, you might choose to have music playing as the audience in entering the venue. The integration of music into the speech presentation itself will be determined by the exact nature of the presentation.

On the surface, it does not seem to make sense for the Teach a Kid to Fish presentation to include music beyond a light active music that might play before the speech. The introduction of Patrick Henry, however, might be a good presentation in which to include music. As the speaker offers the introduction, a typical American Revolution era fife and drum might play. As the speech is only a couple minutes long and the music relates directly to the subject matter, this choice would fit perfectly into the presentation.

In deciding to include the fife and drum into the presentation of the introduction of Patrick Henry, the presenter must decide whether to offer live music or music that has been prerecorded. In most cases, prerecorded music makes more sense than having live musicians, but in this case, live musicians would work to enhance the experience for the audience of children.

Some questions to ask if live music will be used:

- Will microphones and amplification be necessary?
- Is there space for live music?
- Will the musicians need to be clothed in a specific manner?
- Will the musicians provide their own instruments?
- If a piano is available and used, will it be tuned before the event?
- Will the musicians rehearse with the speaker before the event?

If prerecorded music is to be used, the presenter will have a number of options to consider in how to deliver the music.

- Music can be prepared as a part of a slide show/PowerPoint presentation, in which case, it would be delivered via computer.

- Music can be loaded onto an iPod® and connected to equipment that would amplify it.

Some questions to ask if you use prerecorded music:

- What equipment is available where the presentation will be done?

- What equipment will you need to provide?

- Will the sound system in the venue need to be managed for the audience to hear the music?

- Who will manage the sound system?

- Who will lower and raise the volume if necessary?

- Can the technology be prepared and tested in advance?

- What will you do if the technology does not operate as planned?

Especially if live music is used, the addition of music to a speech presentation will add a great deal of theatricality. If it is used correctly, music can enhance the audience's enjoyment, understanding and appreciation of a presentation. However, if used incorrectly, music can become a major distraction.

If the music used is out of place and improper, the audience could well spend the whole time wondering why you chose the music you did. If you chose to have a live heavy metal rock band playing while you introduced Patrick Henry, many in the audience would question your choice, and it would become a major distraction.

If the music is too loud, the audience will not be able to hear what the speaker is saying. In this case, it does not matter whether the music choice is correct or not. If your audience cannot hear you, it does not matter what you say or do.

If the music is too soft, it does matter whether there is music at all. If you are going to use music, make sure the audience can hear it and understand why you are using it.

Outside the Box

In many ways, any of the auxiliary tools mentioned above can be considered thinking outside the box when it comes to crafting your speech presentation. Tools such as slide show and PowerPoint have become so much a part of making a presentation that making the presentation with none of the noted auxiliary tools might be considered thinking outside the box. Seating an audience in a circle and walking amongst them as you speak might, at first, seem like a simple no-nonsense way in which to approach a presentation. But as people are so used to sitting in straight rows with a speaker in front of them, the seating itself becomes a tool you can use to engage your audience. The number of these outside the box tools is endless. Using a creative and unique approach to deliver your message can be powerful and, at the same time, dangerous. It can deliver your message instantly, or muddle it so completely that the audience will wonder why they even came. You can shock, amuse, frighten or touch an audience in so many different ways when you consider an outside the box idea to convey your message. Be prepared to test it and practice it numerous times before actually putting it before an audience.

Body language

Having the ability to join your audience, get close to them, actively move about them, and sit with them is an approach that is not for the nervous. To pull this off, you must be comfortable with yourself and your knowledge of your subject matter and presentation. Of course, you also can combine any of the additional tools mentioned earlier with this approach, but your active presence in and around your audience is the most engaging tool you might possess. With this approach, body language becomes a vital outside the box auxiliary tool.

Body language is a tool that you will use whether you plan to or not. Body language can and will convey nearly every emotion you will experience. Being aware of the power of body language and learning to use it to your advantage can be a powerful tool.

Learning and knowing how body language works for and against you can be gleaned by observation. Watching people relate to one another in a live setting is a great first lesson in understanding the power of body language. Do not rely on video or film for this lesson. You need to observe people in a live setting.

Watch how people relate to each other in one-on-one conversations. Watch from a place where you cannot hear what the people are saying to each other. You easily will be able to tell the nature of the communication.

Watch practiced speakers addressing a crowd. People that have spoken to large groups in public for some time usually have a relaxed handle on body language, sometimes without even knowing it.

Watch people that do not speak the same language communicate with each other. When the common bond of language does not exist, body language becomes a pronounced and important part of communication.

As you begin to think about your presentation, think about the nonverbal signals you are sending to your audience. Those watching you register every movement and action you take.

A good example of the power of nonverbal communication is a yawn. The conveyance of this signal to a large audience is infectious. Even a hint of a yawn will quickly spread that heavy feeling through a receptive audience.

The most important device in your arsenal of presentation-giving tools is physical energy. Your physical and vocal energy is more vital than any PowerPoint, video or live action presentation you might offer.

Knowing how to develop what often is referred to as physical presence might well be the most important out-of-box tool at your disposal.

Playing the audience

Playing your audience can mean several things. The term playing the audience can refer to the action of being a good listener and responding to the needs of an individual audience. As a speaker, you should develop this skill and use it every time you speak or make a presentation to a group. Playing the audience also can refer to a presentation in which the speaker plans beforehand to actively include the audience in the presentation.

Planning to include your audience in your presentation can be done on many different levels. The simplest way is to hold a question and answer session after your presentation. This is a standard way to get the audience involved in helping to clarify and spread your message.

An even simpler take on the standard question and answer session is one in which you, the speaker, pose some questions to the audience. This approach will, more often than not, lead to more questions from the audience.

An example of questions that the Teach a Kid to Fish presenter could include in the presentation to the assembled parents in their meeting might be:

1. What, if any, are the barriers that make it difficult to feed your child healthy foods and to be physically active?

2. Does your child walk to school? If not, why not? What barriers, such as distance, are preventing this?

3. What do you feel is the role of schools in the childhood obesity epidemic? Who would you like to receive information regarding your child's weight status, nutrition, and physical activity habits (in some cases this information is received by school health officials, teachers and in some cases administrators)?

All of these questions directly relate to the mission, vision, and goals of the organization and are directly in line with the subject matter requested by the parent/teacher organization that invited Teach a Kid to Fish to present.

Playing the audience in this manner can ensure an extremely dynamic presentation. Addressing an audience in this manner actively shows them that their views are important to you.

To enhance this manner of presentation, it is important to act as an active listener. Active listening is the practice of asking questions based on the responses given by the respondents. To do this, you use the provided questions as a starting point and ask follow-up questions specific to the replies. In this way, the presentation becomes more of a conversation rather than one in which you stand at a podium and speak to the assembled audience.

Adding this tool to your standard presentation can make an evening quite fulfilling for you and the audience. Adding these types of questions to the Teach a Kid to Fish presentation helps the audience understand what the organization is about as it helps the organization understand the needs of the community.

To develop a presentation in this manner, keep a list of questions you might consider asking your audience as you write your main presentation. When adding these questions to your primary presentation, it is best if they are added to the end of your presentation, as they can tend to take over an evening, and you could lose the opportunity to finish your standard speech.

You may consider using questions to lead in to your presentation. This strategy is often a good way to break the ice and build rapport with your audience. The danger with this strategy is that questions often can tend to expand into lengthy discussions and it may be difficult to get back into your primary presentation.

Whether you plan to include questions to the audience at the beginning or end of your presentation, it is suggested that you have a monitor planted in the audience in case the questions get overly long or off topic. If you feel as if you have a good handle on the audience and are adept at steering the conversation back on track, you might do without this assistance. A monitor, such as your host, can help you to lead the audience back to the primary focus of your speech if you discuss this strategy with a monitor before you begin. You might have a question that the monitor can ask that will lead you into your presentation.

Being creative outside the Box

There are endless possibilities of presentation formats you might consider depending on the nature of your presentation, the setting, the audience, and what it is you want to accomplish and leave the audience with. If you are looking to take your presentation to a place where no presentations have gone in the past, start by thinking about presentations you have seen. Ask yourself what has and has not worked with them. Ask yourself what you have enjoyed and taken from those presentations and what caused you to sit squirming in your seat.

If you want to consider a novel speech presentation, consider the audience that will attend the presentation you are crafting. Will the audience be responsive to something outside the box? Some-times, if a presentation is just so out there it confuses those in attendance, the presentation will be remembered as being weird, but the message might be missed. The audience did not report not liking the presentation. They just do not remember what it was about. Be sure you are not pitching your speech over the head of your audience.

If you consider a presentation style that is different from any-thing the audience might be expecting, be sure to run your idea by the person that asked you to speak. Ideally, that individual can be honest enough to tell you if your outside the box idea is good or too far outside the realm of audience comprehension.

Knowing How to Use Your Tools

When you decide to create a presentation that calls for the use of any of the auxiliary tools described in this chapter, be sure that you are well versed in the strengths and weaknesses of each tool you use before you stand in front of 25 people to deliver your speech. If you are a beginner to the world of public speaking, knowing how to employ the tools that you have (voice, mind, body) can be a bit overwhelming without having to worry about what to do if your laptop will not communicate with a projector.

If you do choose to go with a PowerPoint presentation to enhance your speech, plan well in advance of your deadline so you will be completely comfortable with any of the technology you need to help you. Review the questions suggested in this chapter for each of the tools to help prepare yourself. Communicate with the parties involved in helping you put your presentation together on a regular basis, and ask any question that comes to mind so you can be sure of a smooth presentation.

Auxiliary tools can be a great help in enhancing your speech and making it a dynamic presentation that will deliver your message clearly. Be sure, though, that you do not allow the tools to get in the way of that message. Knowing your tools and how to use them before you take the stage will ensure your presentation goes smoothly and that the audience remembers your message.

CASE STUDY: MARTY VAN WESTEN

Marty Van Westen
Nebraska

I spent much of my time doing public speaking as a part of the scholastic forensics competition. After spending eight years competing on both a high school and collegiate level, I now am an assistant coach for a college forensics team in Nebraska. Most of the speeches I gave were public address speeches, including informative, persuasive, analytical, and extemporaneous speeches, which required preparing a speech with a limited amount of time.

I believe that an effective speech should be able to accomplish the message you are trying to convey, as well as be done in an effective manner. A good speech is also organized, so that people can clearly understand what you are communicating. Also, the topic selection is important, especially depending on the audience that you are speaking to.

I would engage my audience by using fun and/or interesting attention-getting devices, which draws an audience into being interested in your topic. I also would use a lot of personal energy when communicating with the audience.

Some of the best ways to engage your audience is by using attention-getting devices. These are small stories or situations, light-hearted, humorous, or deep, that give a small preview of the thesis of the speech, as well as provide a good way to link to what you are talking about.

One of the most common mistakes that inexperienced speakers make is that they are not comfortable with their topic. You need to be comfortable with what you would like to talk about. Other mistakes include being unclear in what you want to say, stumbling too much over your words and not knowing what you want to say next.

Listening is very important as a speaker. By listening to other speakers, you can learn different ways to give your speech, as well as being able to see how to deliver a speech effectively. You also can learn how different audiences react with other speakers, so you can learn how to analyze audiences for what you are speaking about.

I had a fear of being in front of other people giving a public speech, but I was able to overcome it using various techniques. First, you have to know that most people aren't out there to make you feel bad about yourself, and that it will not kill you to be up there. Second, you can overcome the fear by mentally visualizing yourself in a relaxing place, where you feel comfortable being yourself. Lastly, I feel the best way to conquer the fear of public speaking is by just being yourself. If you feel good about what you are doing, then you shouldn't be afraid to just go and do it.

I think the best way to help alleviate the fear of public speaking is to just get in control of your emotions and your fears. By knowing what you want to speak on and what you need to do, you never will have any problems conquering your fears. I feel that visualization is the best way to combat nervousness. Visualize a very comforting place (a beach, your chair in your living room), and imagine that you are giving the speech in that place.

The biggest piece of advice I can give novice public speakers is to just relax and be yourself. People would rather see someone who looks comfortable with him or herself and who is very organized in how he or she gives the speech. If you know what you want to do, then there is nothing you need to worry about.

Chapter 7

The Setting

hen you are asked to give a speech presentation, one of the first questions you will want to ask, after you learn what it is you will be speaking about and who you will be speaking to, is where will you be speaking. Knowing where you will be speaking will help you to figure out how you will go about crafting your presentation.

If you are new to public speaking and will be creating a presentation from scratch, it is important to learn how to create a presentation that is adaptable to many different types of venues, but knowing the specifics of a particular venue is vital to the success of a presentation.

If you have prepared a presentation that might work well in a small classroom and you arrive at a venue where you will be on a large stage in a auditorium, you will have to scramble to adapt, because what works well in a small classroom might not work in that auditorium.

This chapter will look at the many different locations a speaker may be asked to present in. It will describe the strengths and weaknesses of each environment. Also, the chapter will look at how the presenter can use the environment to its best advantage in preparing and delivering a presentation. The chapter also will offer tips on how best to adapt a presentation for delivery in a wide variety of venues.

Beyond the types of venues you might be asked to present in, also consider the setup of the venue. The venue setups will vary from an elevated stage with seating in front of you such as you might find in a theater, to being in the middle of a small classroom with attendees seated in desks or chair all around you.

You can be part of a community type presentation where you are literally part of the audience, or you might find yourself in the dark behind the audience delivering your presentation while a slide show plays on a screen in front of the audience.

A short list of the types of venues you might be faced with as you go out into the public speaking world includes:

- Auditorium
- Gymnasium
- Classroom
- Religious area
- Reception/meeting hall
- Restaurant
- Park

Each of these particular venues has its strengths and weaknesses and can be a desirable location (or not) for your presentation depending on what your presentation is. For example, if you are delivering a speech presentation on the importance of parks to the health and well-being of a community, you might be well advised to make your presentation in a park as opposed to making it in a dark studio. Here we will explore each of these common venues, describe what you might face if you should be asked to present a speech in one and look at its strengths and weaknesses.

The Venue

The venue, or the location of your presentation, will have a great impact on how you prepare for your speech. The more technical elements you have in your speech, the greater impact the venue will have on your presentation. The following description of common venues can help you ask the right questions as you prepare your speech presentation. Here are some basic questions that can should be asked of most venues:

- How large is the venue?

- What kind of seating will the audience be in?

- How will the seating be configured?

- What kind of sound equipment will be used? (Podium microphones [mics]? Handheld mics? Clip mics? Headset?)

- How should the presenter prepare for the use of mics?

- Will projection equipment be available if needed? If so, what should the presenter need to connect with this equipment?

- Who will operate the PowerPoint/slide presentation if one is used?

- Will the presenter have time before the presentation to become familiar with the venue and its technology?

- If projection is used, will the lights need to be dimmed to accommodate audience viewing?

Auditorium

An auditorium is a venue, usually with a stage. Because auditoriums are designed and built to stage presentations, they generally are equipped to offer many of the technological tools your presentation might require. Well-equipped auditoriums will have sound and lighting equipment, projection equipment, and good sight lines for audience, and they will be well suited for speakers.

Auditoriums, whether they are stand-alone venues or affiliated with schools, often have tech staff that will be able to answer any questions you have regarding the use of the available technology, but they also might have personnel available to operate that technology for you. If this is the case, be sure you provide them with foolproof instruction regarding your needs.

What an auditorium offers in space and equipment, it might lack in intimacy. Smaller auditoriums (200 seats) can be somewhat intimate, but putting a speaker on a stage raised or separated somehow from the audience can give the speaker a removed quality. In such cases, the speaker must work a little harder to connect with the audience and create a sense of intimacy. This can be accomplished by talking directly to the audience, asking for an audience response of some kind at the beginning of a presentation, coming down into the audience, or bringing some part of the audience onto the stage. In theater, this is called breaking the fourth wall and refers to breaking through the separation between performers and audience. The larger the auditorium, the more difficult this task it to accomplish but not impossible.

Another weakness of such a venue is also one of its strengths. When a venue has the type of technological equipment well furnished auditoriums have, it is often hard not to employ that equipment. Lighting, sound and projection capabilities offer the presenter the opportunity to enhance the presentation in such a way as to make it a dynamic and attractive stage show. Such actions also can get in the way of a clear and concise message-oriented speech. As we discussed in the last chapter, technology can get in the way of a good message and does not always operate smoothly. Before flashy lighting tempts you, make sure you have your message clear and your basic speech down pat.

If you have been asked to give a presentation in an auditorium, there are some specific questions about the venue to ask as you begin to prepare your speech:

- Will the audience be in the house or on the stage? (Often, if a large auditorium is used for a smaller speaking engagement, the audience will be on stage with the speaker, giving the presentation a much more intimate quality.)

- How large is the stage?

Gymnasium

A gymnasium is a common venue for many different types of presentations. Presentations for your classmates, community organizations, and sports and performing arts organizations might be held at your school gymnasium. Gyms are large open spaces that can accommodate many people in a variety of seating configurations. Sometimes, raised stage platforms are used, but usually, however, the gym is just a big open space in which folding chairs are set up for audience and the presenter is situated on the same level.

Whether the speaker is in front of the audience in a gym or the audience is seated on a circle, gyms can offer quite an intimate setting as the speaker is on the same level as and a part of the audience in attendance. It is easy for the presenter to move among the audience and to speak quite directly to and with the audience in a gym. This is the greatest strength of such a venue.

The greatest weakness of a gym is usually sound quality. The acoustics of a gym often make difficult to hear and understand a speaker. Even if a microphone assists your speech, the acoustics of most gyms make it difficult to hear or understand speech. To overcome this venue weakness, it is vital that you speak clearly and distinctly.

Though it is not necessarily a weakness, you will find that many gym venues are not technically well-endowed. Technical equipment such as microphones, amplifiers, projectors for slide presentations, and a projection screen have to be brought in. If the gym is in a school, the school probably will have this equipment. Be sure all of the equipment is tested before the presentation.

If you have been asked to give a presentation in a gymnasium, you should ask a number of questions about the venue as you begin to prepare your speech:

- Is there a stage or a raised platform from which to present?

- How large is the stage?

Classroom

In many ways, classrooms are the perfect setting for speech presentations because that is what they are designed for. Classrooms are intimate, and it is easy for a speaker to address an attending audience directly. Most classrooms are sound acoustic venues in which you will have little problem being heard. Most classrooms can accommodate any auxiliary tools you might use to assist you in telling your story or sending your message.

The venue weaknesses with classrooms might be that the space can be rather cramped. If you are in a small classroom with 50 of your classmates all gathered to hear your speech, they might be uncomfortable. You might not be able to do much about this other than to make light of it and keep your presentation short.

If you are giving a presentation in class (which is probably the most likely scenario for most students), you should ask a number of questions about the venue as you begin to prepare your speech:

- How large is the classroom?

- How many people will attend?

Sanctuary

It is not uncommon to be asked to speak in a religious space. Many different types of secular, non-secular, community focused, political, educational meetings, conferences, and presentations are held at religious buildings, like churches or synagogues. Sanctuaries share many of the same strengths that classrooms do in regard to speech presentations in that they are venues that were designed and built to be speaker friendly.

Sanctuaries offer a wide array of configurations and sizes. Some sanctuaries are as small as 50 seats while large sanctuaries can be several thousand seats. They might be large open spaces with flexible seating configurations or more theatrical in design with raised stages before seating that is low in front and gradually rises as it gets further back.

Sanctuaries will also vary widely as regards to technical equipment. Well-equipped sanctuaries will offer all the bells and whistles that well-equipped auditoriums will have. They will be equipped with high-end sound systems, lighting, and projection equipment that will give you the ability to carry off just about any kind of presentation you can create.

The great strengths of most sanctuaries are that they are acoustically well designed for speakers and that they are designed to be intimate, no matter the size. Most sanctuaries have open stages that are close to the gathered people.

The weaknesses of sanctuaries will vary greatly depending on the design and your needs. If you have been asked to give a presentation in a sanctuary, you should ask a number of questions about the venue as you begin to prepare your speech:

- How large is the sanctuary?

- Is there a stage or a raised platform from which to present?

- How large is the stage?

- Is there subject matter that is off-limits out of respect to the denomination of the sanctuary's owners?

Reception/meeting hall

Whether you are giving a toast at a family wedding or speaking to a community group about the importance of TKF, you could find yourself in a reception/meeting hall. This type of hall can be found in hotels, restaurants, churches, schools or community centers. A reception/meeting hall is usually a large open space, much like a gymnasium, but with ceilings that are not as high as might be found in a gym.

Because the ceilings in meeting halls are usually lower than those found in gyms and meeting halls are generally designed to accommodate communication, most meeting halls will not have the same acoustical difficulty that you are likely to come across in a gym. Meeting halls that have high ceilings usually have some other feature that will help to control the sound such as carpeted floors or sound dampening features.

Meeting halls usually have flexible seating and are often equipped with a stage or portable platforms that can be used to raise the presenter. That said, one of the weaknesses of meeting halls that do not have the ability to raise the presenter is that the sight lines sometimes can suffer. People seated some distance from the speaker might have a hard time seeing.

Well-equipped meeting halls will have all the technical equipment you might need.

If you have been asked to give a presentation in a reception/meeting hall, you should ask a number of questions about the venue as you begin to prepare your speech:

- Is there a stage or a raised platform from which to present?

- How large is the stage?

Restaurant

If you are asked to give a presentation at a restaurant, you had better hope your speech presentation is going to be fun and entertaining or that the restaurant has a reception hall in which the presentation will be given (see above). Restaurants offer so many variables and weaknesses that, unless the presentation is a toast, a short introduction, a comedy routine or a song, you will be fighting noise from all the other restaurant activity happening around you as you attempt to be heard. That said, if you are there for a fun presentation, chances are that the audience will be in a great mood, and you are assured of a happy, receptive gathering.

If the speech presentation is to be given in the restaurant while there are diners not associated with your event, you probably will not need to worry about auxiliary elements such as sound systems and projectors. The presentation is probably a short toast, story, or some other type of light presentation. The most important issue for you, other than exactly what you will say, is being heard.

If you are giving a presentation in a restaurant, there are a number of questions about the venue to ask as you begin to prepare your speech:

- Will the presentation take place in the restaurant eating area or in a restaurant meeting/reception room?

- If the presentation is to be given in the restaurant eating room, will there be other diners not associated with your presentation?

- Is any technical support (microphones, projector, etc.) available if necessary?

- How many will attend?

- Will people be eating during the presentation?

Park

Making a speech presentation outdoors can provide the biggest challenge of all for a speaker. Use this section to help plan for any outside presentation whether it is in a large city park or in a backyard. It is here that you should remember the old saying, "expect the unexpected." Even if you are giving a speech in a park or an outdoor area you are familiar with, the number of variables you have to deal with is endless.

The list of variables to keep in mind as you prepare for an outdoor presentation includes weather (heat, cold, rain, snow, wind, dust, lightning, etc...), noise (traffic, airplanes, kids, etc...), animals (dogs, bugs, birds, bats), and any audience distraction you can possibly imagine. That said, if you are prepared to deal with these issues, presenting outside can be a wonderful experience.

If the setting of your presentation is a larger area such as a park and you will be speaking to a large group of people, you probably will need a sound system. This is an auxiliary tool provided by your host. Being heard in a large open-air environment is probably the biggest challenge of giving a speech presentation outdoors. Whether you are provided with a microphone or not, when speaking outside, speak extremely clearly and slightly slower than your normal rate of speaking.

If you have been asked to give a presentation in a park or other outdoor venue, there are a number of questions about the venue to ask as you begin to prepare your speech:

- Is there a stage or a raised platform from which to present?

- How large is the stage?

- Is the stage covered?

- Will the audience be sheltered?

- What will be done in the event of bad weather?

- How will the natural light affect the projection equipment if used?

Working the Room

No matter what type of venue you are preparing to give a speech presentation in, the audience, their relation to you, and what you are saying should always be your primary focuses. For that reason, be aware of the size of the audience and the configuration of the seating in the venue. Knowing these facts will help you prepare a strategy for relating to those gathered to hear your message.

It is the rare individual that can go into any situation unprepared and win the audience over with charm and charisma. Knowing exactly what you are preparing for can lend a certain amount of comfort that will help you to develop a relationship with the audience before the presentation even begins.

Relating to the audience and helping them relate to you is called working the room. Achieving this skill takes time and comfort with your material. How the audience is arranged has a lot to do with how you relate to them and they to you. What follows are some common audience configurations and some tips on how you, the speaker, can help yourself work the room in a more comfortable and familiar manner.

Theater stage

For those speakers new to making public presentations, making a presentation from a theater stage to a large gathering can be either the easiest entry to public speaking or the most difficult. Some find that speaking from a stage is easy because the speaker is removed from the audience and, in many instances, cannot even see those in attendance because of stage lights. Other speakers find this to be an odd, even frightening, position to be in.

If you are in the first group and are comforted by not being able to see your audience, you must remember that they are there. You still will be able to hear them. The greatest danger in not being able to see your audience is that you cut yourself off from them and turn the experience into an impersonal exercise in talking at a wall. It is vital that you form a relationship with your audience.

There are several ways you can work the room in a situation where you are to speak to a group, large or small, from a theater stage.

- Mingle in the lobby before your presentation — introduce yourself and your organization to those in attendance. This may help comfort you if you are nervous about speaking to people.

- If you are speaking from behind a podium, come out from behind the podium and step to the foot (front) of the stage, closer to the audience.

- Ask that the house lights of the auditorium be kept at a level to accommodate your seeing the audience.

- Make sure there is some give and take in your presentation where you ask the audience questions early on. Do not wait until the Q&A session at the end of the presentation.

In-the-Round

You might encounter a configuration in which audience seating is set up with you, as a speaker, as part of a large circle or in which you are the center of a circle (or square) and are completely surrounded. Like the theater setting, such a configuration either will be a great thrill or another extremely frightening proposition.

The strength of having your audience in-the-round is that you are assured of an intimate setting in which you are a part of the audience. You probably will not be behind a podium. A room configured in this manner provides a much more intimate setting than that of a space with a theater stage.

The weakness of this configuration is that it makes using auxiliary tools such as slide shows and video difficult. It is possible to use these tools in such a setting, but it takes a certain amount of planning, especially if the audience is relatively large. Moving a few seats in a group of 50 to 100 people is not difficult, but if you find yourself in a larger in-the-round setting of several hundred fixed seats, the PowerPoint presentation you planned will be difficult to pull off.

If you are asked to give a presentation in an in-the-round setting, you should ask a number of questions:

- How large an audience will be expected?

- Is the seating fixed or can the chairs be moved?

- Will the audience be seated at tables?

- Will the presentation be delivered from the middle of the circle or will the presenter be a part of the circle?

Whether you are a part of the circle or audience surrounds you, make it a point to address the entire gathering. Do not forget there are people behind you who are just as interested in what you are saying.

Three-quarter thrust

For presenters who are comfortable with their audiences and enjoy working in more intimate settings, venues that offer three-quarter thrust stages are ideal. A three-quarter thrust is a configuration in which the audience is set up in a half circle or three-quarter square and the presenter is in the open side of the configuration.

A three-quarter thrust setup allows a speaker to be close to the audience and allows for the use of auxiliary tools such as video or slide shows, though the audience seated to the extreme sides of the configuration might have a difficult time seeing unless the screen is set back. Ideally, there is room enough behind the speaker to allow for a set-back screen if necessary.

Three-quarter thrust configurations can be set up in venues with flexible seating such as meeting/conference rooms, gyms and even outdoors in parks. The configuration is desirable for presentations in which the audience will be engaged with the speaker and one another in Q&A, debate or discussion.

The weakness of the configuration will arise if the audience size is large and the seating and speaker are on one level. In this case, bad sight lines could become an issue.

Speaker's Point:

Do not be afraid to ask as many questions as you possibly can concerning the venue you will be speaking in, the configuration of the audience and the auxiliary tools available to you. If you will be speaking in a situation where the seating is flexible, do not be afraid to ask that the seating be arranged in a particular manner. Asking these questions and making such requests as early as possible can help you to create the most effective presentation possible. In many cases, you will not be able to control the seating configuration, as it will be fixed or be set as per the needs of the event. Knowing the situation as early as possible can help you to be a more comfortable speaker.

Chapter 8

Practice

*N*ow that you have written the presentation, it is time to practice delivering it. Chapter 8 will go over several rehearsal techniques, as well as ways of gathering feedback from rehearsal "audiences" that can help to strengthen the presentation. Here you will explore the use of audio and video as rehearsal tools. Also, you will learn how to use volunteers to help in presentation prep as practice audiences. The practice audiences will have things to watch for, such as clarity of message, clarity of vocal delivery, pace of delivery, and other presentation specific keys. The issue of stage fright also will be addressed. You will discover how to overcome public speaking fright and phobia by being prepared, rehearsed, and ready for a number of unforeseen circumstances such as dry mouth, sweating, trembling, and other signs of fear.

One important step to becoming a great speaker is listening to speakers yourself. Listening to others speak can help guide you to strategies that work and those that do not work. Make a point of going to hear other people that speak in public. Make note of what you think is effective about what you hear. Do the same as you interact with people in public. Make note of the variety of ways people effectively, or not so effectively, communicate with others.

Practice Makes Perfect

The old saying "practice makes perfect" is true. Whether you play the saxophone, volleyball, or deal in slight-of-hand card tricks, you need to practice. A veteran third baseman needs to practice every bit as much as a 10-year-old Little Leaguer. Practicing keeps the fundamentals of what you are doing sharp. Practicing helps keep your mind and body in tune, and it helps you discover new skills. Practicing is a skill and a discipline in itself. To get better at practicing, one needs only to practice regularly. Practice also can be the first step in dealing with stage fright. Stage fright is the fear of being in front of a group of people. Being well practiced, or practiced to the point where your presentation is almost second nature will help you to be more comfortable delivering your presentation in public.

A saxophone player might not necessarily be in rehearsal for a concert, but his or her practice may involve playing scales. A baseball player will practice the fundamentals of fielding ground balls and batting. A writer writes on a daily basis, whether it is a journal or a novel. These are all considered practice.

A public speaker can choose to practice the skill of speaking in many ways. The primary piece of advice for the "how" in this instance, like Nike, Inc. says, is "Just Do It."

You can speak in club meetings, in groups of friends, or in class. The trick with speaking at functions such as these is to be mindful of your speaking but not to appear to the listeners as if you are "practicing on them." Instead, just be mindful of your speech habits and tendencies.

- Do people generally understand things you explain to them?

- Do listeners hear you easily without having to say, "What?"

- Do you seem to easily hold people's attention?

As listening is just as important a skill to public speakers as speaking, you also need to be mindful of your skills in this regard.

- Do you find yourself listening intently to what others are saying to you?

- Do you often ask questions of other speakers that will urge them to flesh out ideas and thoughts?

- Do you find that others share their thoughts easily with you?

Being aware of your communications skills, both listening and speaking, is the first step to becoming a better public speaker. Being honest with yourself is a good start in developing a way of practicing that will support your quest to be a better communicator.

You can start on this quest by taking a week or two to develop your communications mindfulness. Take time each day to make note of your observations about your own communications habits. Refer to the questions asked above and begin a notebook in which you honestly list your strengths and weaknesses as a speaker and listener. Developing your self-assessment is a great way to start improving your skills.

Talking to Yourself

In Chapter 5 when you were involved in the process of writing your presentation, one of the suggestions to strengthen the presentations was to read each draft aloud and record it. Listening to the recordings of these readings is a great tool that can be used not only to help strengthen the presentation draft but also to strengthen your skills as a speaker.

Recording yourself reading should be done in a relaxed manner without the threat of distractions such as ringing cellphones, barking dogs, or loud friends. Put yourself in a place where you can record your voice as you might speak into a microphone on a stand. This is done so you can stand in a relaxed manner and read a text you have prepared for yourself. Ideally, the text should be on a music stand or some other freestanding device to hold the text copy. It is not necessary that the text be a draft of a speech you are writing, any text will do to begin with.

Before you begin, do a couple of sound checks with your recording device. Start recording and speak a few sentences from your text, ad-lib, or just say the A-B-Cs!

Stop the recorder and listen for quality of recording to determine the distance of the recorder from yourself; if the recorder is picking up your voice; are there any background noises that will affect your recording?

After you are sure you will get a quality recording, start the recorder and read from your chosen text. Plan to read for five minutes. After five minutes, stop the recording and listen to the playback. How does it sound?

- Can you hear every single word?
- Is every single word and sentence fully formed?
- Is there variety in your speech pattern?

You should begin to explore these three fundamental questions.

Can you hear every single word?

If the audience cannot hear every single word you speak, they will lose additional words as they wonder, "What did she say?" Words and sentences are lost when the volume of speech is too low or the words are garbled. Technical issues might play into this scenario as well, but for now, we will focus on your instrument: your voice.

As you are mindful about your speech habits, try to discern where your voice comes from in your body. When you are tense and not mindful about how you are speaking, your voice is probably coming from your throat. Speaking for a long time with your voice in your throat will cause a lack of volume and give you a sore throat.

Proper speaking technique calls for you to support your voice from your diaphragm. Your diaphragm is a large muscle that is located between your lungs and your abdomen. Some might instruct you to "breath from your stomach." This advice, while not accurate, is not far from the truth because it asks you to breath from deep down into your lungs — not necessarily take deep breaths, just to breath from deep in your lungs.

If you want to see what it feels like to breath from your diaphragm, lie on your back on the floor. Take several breaths and then count to 10 aloud, projecting your voice to the ceiling. Your normal way of breathing as you lie on your back is to breathe from your diaphragm. You can breath from higher up in your lungs while in this position, but you have to think about it and force it to happen. Likewise, you can watch a baby lying on its back breathing. You will notice that the baby's stomach rises and falls. This baby is breathing from its diaphragm. This method of breathing is best to support a voice to help it be heard and to speak in a relaxed voice that will not strain your throat.

As you focus on breathing from your diaphragm, you also can focus on opening and relaxing your throat. You can start to focus on these two points as you are lying on the floor breathing from your diaphragm. As you breath, let your mouth relax open and vocalize an "ahhhhh." If you are relaxed and breathing from your diaphragm, the "ahhh" will be relaxed and well supported.

Being mindful of your breathing and the feeling of a relaxed vocalization in this instance might be the most important step you can take toward being an effective speaker. The feeling of well-supported breathing, relaxed vocalization, and over-all relaxation all should be noted and remembered as you move forward.

Is every single word and sentence fully formed?

One of the most common mistakes made by speakers is not speaking full words. When we speak to each other in everyday speech, we commonly drop beginnings and ends of words. In everyday speech, this is usually not a great problem because we are used to doing it; we are used to hearing it; and we are used to understanding (or believing we understand) what is being said. How often have you stood in line at a hamburger place to be asked, "Wha' da ya have?" Translation: What will you have?

As you listen to the recording you made, you can note whether your words and sentences are fully formed. Common lapses of speakers are dropping consonants at the beginnings and ends of words. Changing vowels at the ends of words to other vowels. Turning two words into one word. An example of all three lapses might be "Sidown. I think I love ya," which translates to "Sit down. I think I love you."

Dropping beginnings and endings of words in public speaking tells the audience that the speaker is lazy. Like not being heard, more words are lost as the audience asks itself, "What did he say?"

To enunciate means to speak clearly. Enunciation is vital to clear speech. To practice enunciating your speech, you can try a variety of different exercises.

To begin practicing enunciation, your mouth must be properly warmed up. The same way that a runner stretches before running, warm up your mouth and face before speaking.

Start your warm-ups by stretching your face. To stretch your face, open your mouth as wide as possible and stick out your tongue. Hold this position for a count of five and then close your mouth and scrunch up your face, like you have just eaten a sour lemon, and hold this for a count of five. Repeat these two facial gestures five times.

Continue your warm-ups by standing up straight and breathing in a relaxed manner from your diaphragm. After a minute or two, as you exhale vocalize a soft "ahhh." Do this for about a minute. After a minute, transform the "ahhh" into a "maaah," remembering to support the vocalization from your diaphragm. Repeat "maaah, maaah, maaah" three or four times. Let the "maaah" become "ta-aah" and repeat. Let the "taaah" become "laaah" and repeat.

You can continue your vocal warm-ups by adding a variety of exercises that will warm up and stretch your mouth and voice. You can vocalize "tee too," "bee boo," "kee koo," and any other consonant and vowel combinations such as "lay lee," "way wee," and "soo say."

Tongue twisters and short bits of verse can be added to your warm up. Try this common vocal warm-up verse:

What a to-do to die today, at a minute or two to two;

A thing distinctly hard to say, but harder still to do.

We'll beat a tattoo, at twenty to two

A rat-tat-tat- tat-tat-tat- tat-tat-tattoo

And the dragon will come to the beat of the drum

At a minute or two to two today, at a minute or two to two.

Another fun warm-up verse is:

> *Give me the gift of a grip-top sock,*
>
> *A clip drape shipshape tip-top sock —*
>
> *Not your spinslick slapstick slipshod stock,*
>
> *But a plastic, elastic grip-top sock.*
>
> *None of your fantastic slack swap slop*
>
> *From a slapdash flash cash haberdash shop;*
>
> *Not a knickknack knitlock knock-kneed knickerbocker sock*
>
> *With a mock-shot blob-mottled trick-ticker top clock;*
>
> *Not a rucked up, puckered up, flop top sock,*
>
> *Nor a super-sheer seersucker rucksack sock;*
>
> *Not a spot-speckled frog-freckled cheap sheik's sock*
>
> *Off a hodgepodge moss-blotched scotch-botched block;*
>
> *Nothing slipshod, drip drop, flip flop, or glip glop;*
>
> *Tip me to a tip-top grip-top sock.*

When you are using these or any other vocal tongue-twister warm-ups, the key is not necessarily to recite them as fast as possible, but to be sure that you enunciate them clearly. The more you practice them, the quicker your recitation will become, but clarity is the key.

Finally, read your speech while over-emphasizing every word. As you become more and more familiar with your speech, this might become more and more difficult to do as you vocally slide over commonly used words such as "the," "with," "a," and "to."

Over-enunciating a speech can be as dangerous as not enunciating as the audience will wonder, "Why is she speaking like that?" Over-enunciating as an exercise, though, will help you learn the speech and understand proper speech techniques.

One more word on enunciation and pronunciation: If you are uncertain about the pronunciation of certain words, go out of your way to discover the correct pronunciation. You will remember the story in Chapter 4 concerning John F. Kennedy's pronunciation of the word "Berliner." Kennedy might have been battling his Boston accent, but if you do not want the audience to think you are talking about jelly doughnuts when you are talking about residents of Berlin, learn how to pronounce your words properly.

Is there variety in your speech pattern?

Nothing will bore an audience quicker than a string of sentences that all have the same vocal pattern. In your early preparation for practicing, you listened to the way people speak to one another in everyday conversation. What you heard was a wide variety of sentence shapes with upward inflections being spoken by excited people, downward inflections by bored or tired people, people speaking quickly, and people speaking slowly. You heard people speaking quickly that slowed down to draw out specific words to highlight them. You heard a great variety of speech patterns, often produced by a single speaker.

If these people were to stand before a crowd to recite a text or make a speech, you might hear many of these same people lapse into a repetitive drone of sentence after sentence spoken in the same way, all with downward inflections. This is a common habit in many untrained public speakers. People will fall into this pattern when they are not prepared to speak. They are not prepared vocally or physically, or they are not comfortable with the text of their speech. People fighting stage fright will fall into repetitive speech patterns because they are not thinking about the effectiveness of the speech as they focus on their fright.

Chances are that as you listened to the first recordings you made of yourself reading the text of your speech, you found your speech patterns to be repetitive and dull. This was probably because you were still not comfortable with your text.

When you are listening to the recording of yourself reading the prepared text, what speech patterns are you looking for? Likewise, when you listen to other public speakers, what should you be listening for?

Variety — Listen for a variety of vocal patterns in the speech. A natural way of speaking indicates that questions end on upward inflections and completed thoughts end on downward inflections. This might be true if you are speaking one or two lines, but over a longer speech, this pattern can get dull. If you listen to engaging speakers, you will hear that many statements end with upward inflections at the ends of statements, particularly statements within paragraphs. A statement that ends with an upward inflection has energy and helps lead the speaker and the listener to the next statement or thought. Statements that end with a downward inflection have a certain finality to them and a ceasing of energy.

Highlight a couple of paragraphs of your prepared text or of a book and record yourself reading the text. The first time through, read the text giving each of the statements a downward inflection.

Listen to the recording and notice how there is not a steady flow of energy throughout the reading.

Record your reading of the text again and only give downward inflections to statements that complete paragraphs. Note the way the energy of the upwardly inflected sentences carry you through the paragraph.

Finishing a statement with an upward inflection does not mean every statement becomes a question. It merely means the vocal energy at the end of the sentence rises rather than falls.

If you listen to people in everyday speech you will notice a great deal of variety in the their vocal patterns. The trick for you, as a public speaker, is to make your prepared speeches as naturally varied as everyday speech. The more natural the speech patterns are, the easier it is for your audience to relate to you and what you are saying.

Your Physical Presence

In the same way that you prepare and practice your vocal presentation, you might consider also practicing the way you stand, walk, and physically deliver your speech presentation.

There is a famous passage in Anton Chekov's play *The Seagull* in which a young actress named Nina says, "I acted without meaning ... I did not know what to do with my hands, or how to stand on the stage, I had no control over my voice. You can't imagine how you feel when you know that you are acting atrociously." This feeling of uncertainty is common to people new to speaking in front of the public, whether they are actresses or public speakers. Not knowing what to do with your hands and feeling that you have no control over your physical and vocal actions is one of the most common fears of being asked to speak in public.

Many people have a number of different physical habits that they display in their dealings with the public on a daily basis. Some people pull on their ear, while others cross their arms when they speak. Some people put their tongue between their lips when they pause in speech, and others tap their toes. Everyone has a habit like this. Each of these habits contributes to your physical presence when you are speaking before an audience. How you view these habits in yourself and how you choose to deal with the habits that you would like to minimize can best be dealt with as you prepare to deliver your presentation, but relaxation and awareness are the keys.

Relaxation is key because many of the habits we develop manifest themselves out of nervousness. By understanding how we best relax, and it varies from person to person, we can begin to get a handle on nervous gestures and habits.

Awareness of our physical habits is best viewed through being able watch ourselves and through the eyes of others. We can watch ourselves on video. Video is a very effective tool in practicing to deliver a speech presentation. We also can ask that those we invite to watch us practice make note of the physical gestures and habits that we may wish to minimize.

Relax!

The most effective way to begin to tackle these feelings of "uncertainty" is to relax. Relaxing is easier said than done, but there are ways to do it. Inability to relax is the key component of stage fright. The nervousness that arises out of stage fright can manifest a whole host of nervous tics, gestures, and physical habits that will act against a speaker.

Do not wait until you are standing off stage waiting to be introduced to speak to begin learning how to relax. Start teaching yourself relaxation techniques long before you stand behind the podium. Learning how to relax in the comfort of your own home will allow you to find the best way for you to relax, and learn how to repeat that process as you do stand backstage waiting to be introduced.

Relaxation can help you on so many different fronts.

- Relaxation will help you conquer stage fright.

- Relaxation will allow you to speak in a well-supported voice.

- Relaxation will allow you to use your physical energy as a tool to help you achieve your goals.

You can call upon many formal techniques to help you find a path to relaxation that will, at the same time, help you harness your physical energy. Sometimes, nervous energy can be channeled for a positive performance. These formal techniques include practices such as yoga, meditation and deep breathing. You might find exercises as simple as walking, stretching, or just lying down useful. Different relaxation techniques work for different people. Your goal is to find one that works for you and then discover a way you can practically employ it in a public setting.

Many public speakers report that the best way to relax is to be fully prepared and comfortable with their presentation.

As you work to prepare and practice your speech presentation, take the following steps, some of which have been outlined previously:

- Prepare a speech presentation you are comfortable with.

- Read the speech to yourself several times in a relaxed setting with no outside distractions.

- Find a quiet place to lie on your back and to focus on your breathing for about 10 minutes.

- Start to vocalize as you are lying on your back breathing from your diaphragm.

- Slowly stand as you continue to vocalize.

- Shake your hands and feet as you continue to vocalize.

- As you shake your hands and feet, add energy to your vocalizations.

- Read your text again being mindful of the energy you built up to as you relaxed and warmed up.

After you complete this exercise, stop for the day. You will return to the same exercise the next day adding an additional practice element: a video camera.

Watching yourself

The second day, before you start your relaxation and warm-up practice, set up a video recorder. It is a good idea to have your text set up on a music stand or some other device that will allow you to have it at about chest level. Do not place the text in front of your face or on a bulky piece of furniture that you can hide behind. The idea is to free your hands of the script but still be able to see yourself on the recording.

Go through your relaxation and warm-up session. Start recording just before you begin to read.

As you read, do so in as relaxed, though energetic, as manner as you can. Because the camera is stationary, you will be confined to a small area in which to move. Do not place any restrictions on yourself with this first reading other than trying to stay within the camera range. Many stage directors will report that the first reading of a text is often the most honest reading. Rehearsal after that is just trying to reclaim that honesty. Though this is not, technically, your first reading, you are for the first time delivering your text to an audience (even if it is just yourself), so it might feel like the first time.

After you complete your reading, make some notes to yourself as to how you felt about what you did. Do not watch the reading for at least several hours, preferably until the following day when you can watch the recording fresh.

When you return to watch the recording, take several kinds of notes over several different viewings. Watch the recording the first time straight through. Do not take notes as you watch, just watch. After your first viewing, make note of your overall impressions. Avoid getting caught up on impressions like, "I look terrible on camera," "My hair is a mess," or "That shirt looks awful on me." This type of overly critical self-judgment is unnecessary and detrimental to the task at hand. Rather, focus on the message and the delivery of the message.

- Did you deliver the speech in a relaxed manner?
- Did you look relaxed in your delivery?
- Were you unnecessarily fidgeting?
- Did you deliver the speech clearly?
- Did you deliver the speech with energy?

Answer these questions honestly, and then go back and watch the recording again. As you watch, pinpoint the places in the speech delivery where you did not seem relaxed. What were you doing that made you not seem relaxed? What parts of the speech were unclear? Where did your energy subside?

Identify the specifics of where and when you felt the presentation was unclear or low on energy. After doing so, make another recording in the same manner. That is, go through your warm-up and preparation and make a recording of your delivery of the speech. This time, watch for some common mistakes such as:

- Leaning on the podium
- Pacing or dancing around
- Standing extremely stiff and unmoving
- Burying your face in the text
- Throwing in unnecessary vocalizations such as "uhhh," "ummm"

An infinite number of other vocal and physical habits possibly can get in the way of your delivery. These mistakes may not seem like a big deal, but they lead to boredom or distraction for your audience.

Leaning on the podium seems like a natural and relaxed action that should not have any effect on the audience. The fact is, the subtle action of leaning on the podium transfers the energy of your body, your physical energy, not to your audience but into the podium. The audience picks up the subconscious message of "low energy" or "lazy."

Pacing back and forth in front of your audience is extremely distracting if it is done without purpose. Speakers that are not standing behind a podium should, unless they have a reason to move, stand still. That does not mean you have to be a tree root with both feet planted, but unnecessarily pacing back and forth will drive an audience to distraction.

Likewise, standing like that tree, rooted and unmoving, will come off as stiff. Stiff will probably have the effect of telling your audience you are either extremely nervous or extremely bored.

Burying your face in your text will bring on a whole bunch of problems with your audience. If you hide behind your text or read directly from your script, your audience probably will feel you do not know what you are talking about. Keeping your eyes glued to your script will transfer most of your communicative energy to your script instead of your audience and the subject of your presentation. If you read directly from your presentation, your audience might feel as if they have been cheated out of their precious time, as they could have read your presentation themselves. Reading directly from your prepared text tells your audience that you are not prepared.

If you are confident enough to get your face out of your prepared text, be prepared enough not to pepper your speech with "uhhhh," "ummm," and the deadly "like" and "you know." Verbal habits such as these tell the audience you might not know, and they will not "like" that.

These are just a handful of mistakes public speakers commonly make and that you should work hard to avoid. If you are prepared and relaxed, your audience will pay attention, and you will be rewarded for your hard work and preparation.

As you watch your recorded self, make careful note of any of these mistakes, or others, that you make. Record yourself several more times and note your improvement. You are relaxed, standing still but not stiff; you are speaking out to the audience; you are not saying "ummmm, you know."

It is now time for a live audience.

Your practice audience

In theater, the "practice audience" is commonly referred to as the "preview audience." Previews are considered rehearsals and audiences attending previews know they are not seeing fully prepared shows. It is not unusual for a show to be in previews for weeks or even months before it officially opens. Previews serve several purposes:

- Previews allow the actors to perform in front of an audience and adjust their performances accordingly. These adjustments vary depending on the type/style of show they are performing.

- Previews allow directors, playwrights, other non-performing members of the creative team to sit with an audience to help judge what works and what does not work. Often, it is difficult for the individuals who have worked so long on a particular show to see the show with fresh eyes. A new audience helps by being those eyes.

- Previews allow word-of-mouth "buzz" to spread, helping to publicize a show before opening.

Your presentation is now ready for a preview in front of a live audience. There are some important considerations about whom you ask to sit in on your initial previews.

- Your preview audience should be made up of people you are comfortable with.

- Your preview audience should include people you know will be honest with you.

- Your preview audience should be made up people who are good listeners.

You can have a preview audience of as many or as few people as you want. Make sure your arrangements are comfortable for you. This preview can be as simple as practicing your speech in front of your mom or best friend. If you suffer from stage fright, you probably want to start with one or two people you are extremely comfortable with and whom you trust.

Your preview can take place anywhere you feel comfortable and have the space to do what you need to do. Space considerations will vary depending on your presentation.

You can run your initial previews with or without any auxiliary tools you plan to use and just focus on the speech. If you have ever heard demo versions of songs that end up as fully orchestrated musical pieces, you might have heard the song performed with only a single acoustic guitar or piano. A demo version of a song is much the same thing as a preview. The focus should not be on all the bells and whistles, just on the message and its delivery.

Try to do some relaxation exercises and vocal warm-ups before your preview audience arrives. The vocal warm-ups are especially important. You can also give yourself a few minutes to relax after your audience is prepared for your presentation.

As your preview audience gathers and before you give your presentation, talk to them about what you want them to consider as they watch your presentation. Do not tell them what you presentation's message is. This is something you want them to get out of the presentation itself. You want your audience to note all of the things you have been working on as you wrote and practiced your presentation:

- Can you hear every single word?
- Is every word and sentence fully formed?
- Is there variety in your speech pattern?
- Did you deliver the speech in a relaxed manner?
- Did you look relaxed in your delivery?
- Were you unnecessarily fidgeting?
- Did you deliver the speech clearly?
- Did you deliver the speech with energy?
- Did you convey the message you meant to convey?
- Was there anything unclear about the message?
- What did the audience particularly enjoy about the presentation?
- What did the audience not enjoy about the presentation?

If a question and answer session will be a part of your presentation, now is a good time to practice that. Let your audience know you will include a question and answer period after your presentation and invite them to think of some questions as they listen.

After you have briefed your preview audience as to what you want them to look for, you can begin your presentation, or you can ask that the audience give you a couple of minutes to allow you to prepare. If you are dealing with stage fright, you will want a couple of minutes.

Now is your opportunity to begin your relaxation exercises. Take a minute to step out of the room to a quiet place. Stand quiet for a minute and focus on what you want to achieve. Focus on the fact that the audience you have asked to assist you with this presentation is there to help you. You will be playing to a friendly house. Take a couple of deep breaths. You are ready to give your presentation.

As you deliver the presentation, you now can start to listen and observe the audience as you make your speech. Because you are avoiding burying your face in your text and you are probably working with a small number of people, make a point of talking directly to your audience. This will not come easily at first, as you will be concentrating on your presentation, but this is a good time to be aware of the audience and to react to the live, in-the-moment feedback you are receiving. As you receive this feedback, make a mental note of it. If you can successfully file this feedback away, you will be able to ask about it when you are through with your presentation.

Practicing Q&A sessions

After you conclude your main presentation, take some time for the Q&A session if that will be a part of your presentation. You should ask that your preview audience ask a question or two that:

A. You do not know the answer to
B. Have nothing to do with what it is you are speaking about
C. Are argumentative

You should be prepared to handle questions of this nature.

If a question is asked that you do not know the answer to, do not attempt to bluff your way through it. Have some suggestions as to where the answer to the question might be found. If a question intrigues you and you would be interested in knowing more about the subject of the question, perhaps you could suggest that you will look into it and you can offer the questioner a way to contact you later to discuss the question.

If a question is asked that you do not know the specific answer to, but you have an opinion on the general subject matter, you can offer your opinion if it is stated as such and if you tell the questioner you do not have a specific answer. In fact, some questions will be asked to which there is no answer. These questions often create further discussion and debate. If there is time to pursue these questions, it is a good idea to do so.

If a question is asked that has nothing whatsoever to do with the subject of your presentation, excuse yourself in a polite manner and attempt to move on. "Thank you for your question, but I'm afraid that I cannot answer that." The most important thing here is to be polite.

If a question is asked that is contentious in nature, begin your response by being polite. If you have a firm answer to the question, answer it. Often, those that ask contentious questions are looking for an argument, and merely asking the question will not satisfy the questioner. If you feel you have answered the question and the questioner continues, you either can continue to answer the question, or you can politely excuse yourself from the exchange by saying something along the lines of, "I appreciate your question and I have attempted to answer it to the best of my ability. If you would like more information…" and you can tell them where they might find further information on the subject. Or, give your excuse as needing to take questions from other members of the audience.

Not getting flustered by difficult questions and questioners is easier said than done. Like making an effective presentation, handling Q&A sessions take a little practice and experience. Be comforted by the fact that those who asked you to speak did so because they believe you have the information they are looking for. Most members of the audience are on your side. Do not be pressured by the need to have all the answers. Nobody does. If you make an honest attempt to answer the questions you know and to help the questioners find the answers to the questions you do not know, you will do fine.

Practice, practice, and more practice

Depending on how comfortable you are with your presentation and delivering it to a live audience, you might consider having several more preview runs. If you decide to do this, consider practicing with a larger audience if possible. Also, try to mix it up with people who have seen the presentation before with people new to your presentation.

If the initial preview presentations you have given focused solely on your delivery and have not included your auxiliary materials such as PowerPoint, video, or music, you should make it a point to have a run-through with these materials and a test audience. These previews will allow you to confirm that your chosen auxiliary materials are clear and easily understood.

If you have the opportunity to practice in a venue similar to the venue you will be speaking in, you might gain a little comfort. If you are able to give an impromptu presentation at a club meeting you are attending, try it. Any opportunity you may have to stand in front of a group of people to practice your presentation, take it.

If you are nervous about speaking in front of a group of people, start small. The more you find and take opportunities to speak in public, the easier it will become.

If you speak in front of groups of people regularly and do so with an easy manner, practicing will keep the fundamentals of the skill sharp. Remember, nobody is so good that they cannot stand a little practice.

Speaker's Point:

You might discover, after previewing your presentation for an audience, that you need to make some changes to the text or the auxiliary materials. These changes should not be made based on the opinions of a single individual, but on trends that become apparent after one or more previews. Remember, the decision to make changes is yours. Do not be afraid to change it or become stubborn about what might believe to true, clear, or important. If you get repeated feedback that something is unclear or needs fixing, consider doing so.

Chapter 9

Preparing to Deliver

re you ready to go? You have written what you believe to be a clear and well-thought-out presentation. You have put together a great PowerPoint presentation that will enhance your message. You have practiced and refined your delivery before several groups of family, friends, and coworkers. What could possibly go wrong?

The fact is, many people get to this point and think they are ready and that the job, aside from the delivery, is done. All they need to do now is show up and speak.

People that think this way often get burned. They show up to the presentation venue and discover that the projector is not working. Worse: They arrive at the presentation site and find they have the wrong flash drive for their PowerPoint presentation. They were told that they would be giving the speech from a stage and arrive to find out that they will be in-the-round surrounded by the audience.

Here we will examine the "day of" the presentation. You will learn points that need to be addressed leading up to the presentation from making sure the technical items work to making sure your voice is functioning properly. We will address the issue of what to do if the needed projector does not work or if the microphone malfunctions. We also will discuss how you, the presenter, can best prepare yourself to deliver a speech. What can you do the day of the presentation to make sure that when you are standing offstage waiting to be introduced, you are certain that everything is in place, and you will be ready to deliver the best, most effective presentation possible?

Preparing Yourself

Now that you have given several preview presentations to friends and family and watched recordings you have made of yourself delivering your presentation, you probably have a pretty good idea as to what you need to do to prepare yourself to deliver your presentation.

Some people will be able to glide seamlessly from their daily life to being on stage giving a presentation in front of their whole school in a relaxed manner. These individuals should, though they do not always, take the time to prepare their vocal chords for such a presentation. Other people suffer greater or lesser levels of anxiety and need to do a little more preparation.

The least you should do to prepare yourself physically to deliver a presentation to a group of people is to warm up your vocal chords and stretch your mouth out to facilitate clear and well-supported speech. Depending on where and when your presentation is in the course of your day, these preparations can take different forms and be done in different places.

If you are in a situation where you can rest your voice the day before or early in the day of your presentation, take advantage of this opportunity. A well-rested voice will perform much better than one that has been active all day.

If you are in a situation where you can do your regular vocal warm-ups a half-hour or so before you give your presentation, do it. Do some deep breathing exercises to warm up your lungs. Go through a series of vocal support exercises as outlined in the previous chapter. Spend some time stretching your mouth and facial muscles and say several well-supported tongue twisters.

If you do not feel comfortable doing these warm-up exercises at the venue you will be delivering your presentation at, you can do them at home or in your office before leaving to deliver your speech. The point is that you should not go into delivering your presentation cold.

If you are somewhat nervous about delivering your presentation, try to find a quiet place to take some deep breaths and relax just before giving your presentation. If you are in a place where you will be on stage, you usually can find a quiet corner to stand still, take a few deep breaths, and prepare. You might use a restroom or a quiet hallway for the same purpose.

Peace of mind, confidence, and self-assurance will come from the preparation you have done before this time. As you take those deep breaths before giving your presentation, know that you have prepared well and that the assembled audience is eager to hear what it is you have to say.

Preparing Your Materials

Finding self-assuredness and confidence comes not only from being physically prepared, but also from knowing your presentation materials are ready. Whether you are presenting a slide show or a musical introduction, make certain before you take the stage that everything is in place and ready to go.

When it comes to making sure your support materials are prepared, the best advice anyone can offer you is: Arrive early. Do not fly in to the venue at the last minute and expect that you will be able to properly set up your PowerPoint presentation or video and be confident that it will run properly. If your auxiliary materials are as simple as a short PowerPoint or video and you have communicated your technical needs to the venue, your setup is as simple as arriving a half-hour early and running through your slides or making sure the video is set and ready to go with the push of a button.

If your auxiliary materials are more complex you will need more time to prepare. Your preparation time will vary depending on the support your presentation will be using. You will, by this time, know what time you will need to prepare. It is vital that you respect your audience and take the time to prepare properly for your presentation.

Essential pieces of your material preparation should be a pen and a clean pad of paper on which to make notes. You might need to make notes as you deliver your presentation. More than likely, you will be thankful for the pen and paper during your Q&A period. The pen and paper come in handy for those multiple question askers as well as any thoughts or ideas that come to mind as the result of a posed question.

If your speech is a short introduction, a toast, or something along those lines, you probably will not require a pen and paper. But be prepared to take notes if you think it might be called for.

Checking it Twice

As presentations will differ depending on their needs, it is impossible to give a checklist for the things that you will need to do to prepare for your presentation. The exact checklist you require will depend solely on the exact nature of your presentation. As you are going through the process of previewing your presentation and making final adjustments to your presentation, make a checklist of the preparations and materials you will need to have on the day of your presentation.

- Directions to venue
- Contact information of host
- Speech notes or script
- Auxiliary materials (if you have a planned slide show or PowerPoint that is stored on a flash drive, consider having a backup, as well)
- Cable or any technical support items you may need
- Relaxation
- Vocal warm-up

Your list may be longer or shorter than this and will depend greatly on the specifics of your presentation. The point is that making a checklist is a great way to decrease the anxiety you might suffer from preparing for and giving a speech presentation. A list can help put everything you need to do in front of you. Your checking things off the list is like erasing a little bit of anxiety with each completed task.

Note that the checklist has the relaxation and warm-up points listed last on the list. It is much easier to relax if you are certain everything else is in place.

A Wrinkle in the Plan

Being fully prepared, relaxed, and having all items completed on your checklist does not mean that all will go according to plan. Part of being fully prepared is being prepared for things that might, and will, go wrong. Planning for things to go wrong does not mean, however, that you should focus on them because that will put a huge crimp on your ability to relax.

It has been mentioned on numerous occasions that you should plan your speech presentation so it can be delivered without the use of auxiliary materials. That is not to say you should leave those materials out all together. You should, however, be prepared to deliver your presentation without them because you will come across instances when the projector will not work, the computer will malfunction, or your flash drive will not be recognized by the computer.

How you deal with the failure of a computer or a late arrival will vary from presentation to presentation, but have a backup plan. The Teach a Kid to Fish PowerPoint presentation used as an example in Chapter 6 is an excellent visualization of statistics that show the growth of the epidemic of childhood obesity in Lincoln, Nebraska. If the presenter came to the point in the presentation in which the various graphs and charts were to be shown and the projector malfunctioned, the presenter would need to be prepared to convey the information presented on the slides. The presenter should not spend any time attempting to fix the projector. The presenter should not utter any words of discouragement regarding the projector or the venue. It is assumed that the presenter checked the equipment before the presentation. If the projector malfunctions, as technical equipment does on a regular basis, it is the presenter's responsibility to carry on.

In the case of the Teach a Kid to Fish presentation, the presenter could have a printout of each of the slides to refer to. The presenter should merely use the printed documents to relate to the audience, "Statistics show that the schools where there are higher percentages of students qualifying for free/reduced meals also show there to be a higher percentage of students identified as overweight or obese." The graphic display of this would have helped make the point, but if the presenter had spent any time at all fighting with the malfunctioning projector, the point would have been lost completely. If the presenter is prepared to carry on without the slides, the audience might never even know that there was a problem.

The example noted above is a relatively simple situation to remedy. That said, auxiliary aids, whether they be slides or videos, should be used to make a specific point.

Any time you add auxiliary aids to your presentation, ask yourself, "What is the main point I am trying to make?" You should also ask, "How can I make the same point if the projector breaks?"

Speaker's Point:

We have all heard the advice to nervous speakers that they should picture the audience in their underwear. This advice is amusing but not that helpful. Think about how flustered you would be if you came out to speak and the audience actually was in their underwear. Better advice might be to imagine your audience relaxed and eager to hear what you have to say. This advice is far more helpful because it is probably true. Focus on knowing that your audience welcomes you, is supportive of you and your mission, and is grateful for your presence.

Chapter 10

The Delivery

f you have taken the time to prepare your presentation ad-
equately, the delivery is assured to be the easiest part of this
entire process. Even if you are a nervous speaker, if you are
well prepared, the presentation will be fun, and the time you are
at the podium will fly by. This chapter will describe what you
can expect as you deliver your presentation. The chapter also describes how you should expect the unexpected. The last chapter
discussed preparing for the unexpected, but now that you are at
the podium and you have a group of gossiping underclassmen in
the audience, you should know what to do. The chapter will discuss how to channel nervous energy while on stage; how to listen
to the audience as the presentation is being delivered; the concept
of delivery "timing"; and how to be aware of your environment.
Often, when preparing to give a presentation, the presenter prepares in an empty space. The space changes dramatically when

it is filled with people. The lighting is different, the sound is different, and the energy is different. This is especially alarming to first-time presenters. You will be guided through what needs to be done to acclimate to the environment of the space as you begin the presentation.

Taking the Stage

Whether you are new to delivering speech presentations or have given so many you've lost count, the most anxious moments come just before being announced. Your mind is racing over a multitude of issues from "I hope that projector works" to "I hope they can't see the zit on my nose," and everything in between. Most of your worries have no basis except to help provide a good boost of energy.

The moment you take the stage to deliver your speech presentation, you have formed a partnership with the audience. Both you and the audience have roles to play. In playing a role, whether in a play or the role you are playing as a speaker, you must deliver your lines and listen to those who are your partners in this event.

The transformation you make as you step to the podium is from the dark of backstage to this moment as you begin to share your message with your community. Whether that community is gathered to hear about your class project on the epidemic of childhood obesity, the introduction of Patrick Henry, or your campaign speech for treasurer of student government, the partnership you are forming with your audience as you take your place can provide you with the energy and confidence you need to deliver your speech well. Your partners want you to succeed.

Finding your light

If you are taking the stage and you will be doing your presentation without a podium, you might need to "find your light." If you are on a large stage in a theater or auditorium, there might be areas of the stage that are lit specifically for a speaker, which also means there will be dark areas. You probably will have been informed of where to place yourself before your presentation, but take half a second as you enter the stage to find the proper location to place yourself.

If you find yourself in a situation in which you have not been informed of where to stand, be sure you are standing in light. The light spot on the stage is usually the warmest spot, and you will feel the light on your face and in your eyes.

Your Speech Presentation

This is what you practiced. Ideally, you will step to the podium, and you will carry on with your presentation in exactly the same manner in which you practiced it. You may be in a different venue with a larger audience, but the ideal is that everything goes exactly as planned and practiced.

The two elements you were not able to control as you practiced your speech presentation that you now face as you step to the podium are the venue and the audience. Even if you were able to practice your presentation in the venue before this moment, the difference now is the audience. A venue takes on a completely different feeling when it is filled with people. As you step to the podium, it is vital that you take stock of the total environment.

If you were step to the podium and deliver the speech exactly as you had the last time you practiced it at home in front of your camera, even though you found your presentation to be flawless at that time, the presentation would be a lifeless bore to your audience. The audience is the difference now. How you relate to your audience in the first moments of your presentation is vital. How you relate to your audience, in many ways, will be decided by the venue.

Creating a bond

It is easier to create a bond with an audience if you are close to them, can look them in the eye, can sit with them, can talk to them nearly one-on-one than if you are standing on a large stage separated from them by an orchestra pit and a large bank of lights. However, in both cases, you must create the bond with the audience immediately.

Creating a bond with an audience can be as simple as standing out from behind the podium, smiling, looking directly at your audience, and introducing yourself. Thank the audience immediately for coming. Relate a common interest.

Being open and welcoming is a great first step. If you are standing out in front of the podium, don't cross your arms. Open body language is very important.

You will feel the energy created as you step on stage. The energy is a combined force of your nervous energy and the energy of the audience. The energy is a positive force you will use to create this bond between yourself and your audience. A smile can be the start of that bond. A "thank you" can be the beginnings of a seal to that bond. The common thread can complete the seal.

An excellent example of a speaker creating a common bond with his audience can be found in Chapter 1 in John F. Kennedy's speech to the people of Berlin. "Ich bin ein Berliner" is a classic case of a speaker creating a strong and emotional bond.

The individual that is introducing Patrick Henry seemingly has a little less to choose from when it comes to finding this common thread, but with a little creativity, he might find that "threads" are the way to go. The audience is a group of 21st century high school students, and so is he. Reference to patriotism and America might be used to create a common bond. Even a bit of humor can help his peers relate to him and welcome him.

Once you have taken the time to create that bond, you can step behind the podium and begin the main speech presentation. You will hold the bond if your presentation is direct, you retain eye contact, and you speak to your audience and not over them, at them, or under them.

Speaking to your audience goes back to the lessons learned in Chapter 3. If you have properly prepared and you know your audience, the delivery of your message is merely a matter of being direct and listening to your audience.

Listen to your audience

In some ways, it seems strange to say that as you go to speak to an audience, you also have to listen. The truth of the matter is that listening is every bit as important as speaking is. Remember, you are part of a two-way communication, and you would be missing out if you did not listen to your audience.

Listening to your audience provides instantaneous feedback as you deliver your speech. It will tell you when you have your audience on the edge of their seats and when they are restless. Listening will tell you when to pause and allow your audience to laugh or react to a point you have made. It provides you with the other half of the conversation.

This is not to say your audience literally will be speaking to you. More than likely, unless you are asking direct questions of your audience your audience will not be speaking. Your audience will communicate with you, though by looking at you, nodding, and reacting to your words. A yawn or glazed look can communicate a lot about your presentation.

You let your audience know that you are listening to them by talking to them in an attentive manner. You probably know what it is like to be in a conversation with someone who is not interested in what you have to say. The individual talks at you, and even if you attempt to speak, they barrel over you and continue talking. You know when someone is speaking with you because he or she is attentive to your feelings, thoughts, and opinions, even if you are not speaking. People listening to you look at you as they speak, pause when you react, and look to you for confirmation of a point.

When you speak to a large group of people, it is important that you speak to them in the same way that you would want to be communicated with. Talk to them as a two-way communication. Listen and speak.

When you listen and speak, you will notice you give unconscious signals to your audience that you are welcoming two-way communication. You honor two-way communication when you allow your audience to react honestly and openly to what you are saying. The audience reacts by applauding, laughing, gasping, and a multitude of other appropriate and, sometimes, inappropriate ways. You honor the audience reaction by not speaking over their laughs or other reactions. You allow them to react.

Put yourself in an audience and listen to how an experienced speaker handles an audience reaction. When the speaker says something that elicits a laugh, the speaker allows the audience to laugh and then pauses until the laugh begins to die down before proceeding. This is called "holding for the laugh." The speaker does not wait until the laugh is completely gone, just until it starts to fade.

Holding for the laugh, sigh, or any other reaction takes a bit of practice that can only come by speaking to a live audience. Holding for the laugh demands that the speaker listen to the audience and allow them to react honestly.

If the speaker did not hold for the laugh, the audience probably would stop laughing because in doing so they would miss what the speaker was saying. The speaker tells the audience in this case that he does not give them permission to laugh. The speaker also tells them he will not allow them to react openly and honestly.

Timing

When, in the course of communication, we refer to the issue of timing, it does not refer the fact that in practice, your speech presentation was five minutes long, and now that you are speaking to an assembled audience, it is taking nine minutes. Timing refers to the pace at which your presentation moves forward in a natural manner allowing for a clear natural delivery and audience interaction.

You will start to grasp the issue of timing when you begin previewing your speech for friends and family. You will notice the change in dynamic from speaking to your recording device to speaking with a live audience. You will notice a change in timing as that audience moves from people you know to a group you do not know.

When you are giving your speech in the beginning of the process and you are reading it only to yourself or your recording device, your focus is only on the words and thoughts of the presentation. You do not need to be think about an audience and their reactions. When you gather people you know to hear your preview presentations, you are speaking to a group of people you know, so you do not need to spend any time creating a bond with them. You even might anticipate their reactions to certain points in your speech. The group is probably smaller than the group you will be speaking to at your planned speech presentation. You will note, however, that the timing and pace of the speech is a little different than when you read it to yourself and your recording device. Likewise, when you start to deliver your presentation to the 400 members of the junior class that may vote for you in the upcoming student government elections, you will note another change in pace. It is up to you, the speaker, to adjust to the change on the spot. The adjustment will come as you listen and react to your audience. Talking to a group of 400 is quite different than talking to a group of four or to yourself and a tape recorder. The timing and the pace will be different.

Environmental Awareness

The stage, the floor of the gymnasium, the audience, the light, and the sound, all of these things constitute the environment of the venue in which you are speaking. Your speech, the slide show, your voice, your nerves are also part of the overall environment of the venue.

Being aware of the total environment of the room in which you are speaking is a skill that will develop in you over time as you experience making speech presentations. One of your tasks as you engage in the activity of making speeches is to be open to the awareness of the total environment. The more open and aware you are as a speaker, the more effective you will be. The more open and aware you are, the better able you will be to handle difficult situation such as people talking during your presentation, bad sound systems and dark stages.

If the question is, "How do you handle a room in which there are six crying babies that are putting a damper on the audience's ability to hear your speech?" The answer will vary from situation to situation. If you know your audience and are aware of the environment in which you are speaking, the issue usually will take care of itself.

The speaker that is not aware of the overall environment and gets flustered by the crying babies will lose control of the situation and consequently lose control of the audience and the speech. In this case, the environment has succeeded in becoming primary focus of the evening and not your presentation.

The speaker preparing to give the presentation for Teach a Kid to Fish knows that he or she is going into a school gym and that the audience will be primarily made up of parents from the PTO. Knowing these two facts alone tells the speaker that the sound will be difficult because it is a gym and there might be more than a few young children in the audience with their parents. To control this environment, the speaker asks the host, probably the Parent Teacher Organization president, if he or she would request that parents remove any disruptive children during the presentation. Or, the presenter might ask that the host speak to parents of children that become disruptive during the presentation. In this way, the presenter sought to control the environment before the environment overtook him or her.

The most positive aspect of your awareness of the total environment is the energy you can gather from it. Nervous energy you hold is good and can be used to your advantage. The energy of the audience, as mentioned earlier in the chapter, can be used to your advantage. Likewise, energy is a part of the total environment that includes your nervous energy, the energy of the audience, the energy of the lights and sound. Knowing the energy in the venue is created by your speech, whether you are introducing Patrick Henry, toasting a newlywed couple, or introducing an organization you volunteer for to a local Parent Teacher Organization, can be a powerful tool you can use to succeed. Again, all you need to know is that everyone wants you to succeed.

 Speaker's Point:

Do not be afraid to pause. James Joyce once wrote: "He laughed to free his mind from his mind's bondage." If you find that you ever get to appoint as you stand before an audience and you feel overly nervous, like you are speaking too quickly, that you have lost your place, or are out of sorts in any way, do not be afraid to pause. Use the pause to "free (your) mind of (your) mind's bondage. If, in the course of your preparation to deliver your speech presentation, you practiced some simple relaxation techniques, pause, take a breath, relax, and remember that everyone wants you to succeed.

Chapter 11

Feedback

I f, in your endeavors as a public speaker, you plan to give more than one presentation, you will need to examine the concept of audience feedback on multiple levels. As discussed in the last chapter, your awareness of the audience will provide you with a good feedback as you deliver your presentation. If you include a question and answer session as a part of your speech presentation, this will provide you with another type of audience feedback. Also, plan to have a post-presentation discussion with your host or teacher to exchange feedback on the presentation.

As you begin to decide what types of feedback you will include in your assessment, you should remember that feedback, like the speech presentation you developed and delivered, is a two-way process. From the audience's point-of-view, they might want more information about your organization or the issue on which you were speaking. From your point-of-view, you will want to hear their ideas about the subject of your presentation to assist you and your organization with further development, and you will want to get an idea from them as to how clearly developed and delivered your presentation was.

Q&A

Question and answer sessions are a great way to exchange information, clarify thoughts expressed in your presentation, and get new ideas from audience members. Q&A sessions are particularly helpful for presentations of an informational nature. If you plan to include a question and answer segment as a part of your presentation, you can plan for it before your presentation by letting the audience know you will be answering questions after the presentation. If you are speaking with a group you are not familiar with, consider enlisting the host or teacher in charge of the event to assist you in identifying questioners and to manage any questioners that get off topic, out of line, or attempt to hijack the proceedings in their own interest.

Some general words of advice regarding Q&A sessions are:

- Be polite, even when you feel pushed not to be.

- Stay on topic, even when your questioners stray off topic.

- Try to keep questioners to one question and a follow-up if there seem to be a lot of questions.

In Chapter 5, you read the draft of the presentation being prepared by Teach a Kid to Fish that was to be delivered to the Parent Teach Organization of a local elementary school. The following are a sample of questions and comments that come up in the post-presentation Q&A session:

I have three daughters that are 'big' but the Doctor tells them that they are healthy. Their size doesn't seem to be causing any other health issues, but the school nurse keeps telling me that they need to see a doctor because they can't participate in gym. Is this the school's business?

My girls always talk about their weight, BMI, nutrition, and activity. Is it healthy for an elementary school girl to be so focused on her weight?

My doctor never mentions BMI. Just gives percentiles. How should I interpret this?

What's considered a normal weight change?

Our doctor is always pushing organic. Organic doesn't mean it's good for you. Eat what you want to eat in moderation.

Our Doctor doesn't talk to us about activity, nutrition, and screen time. Should he?

The school sends home all of this information saying we should eat healthier and get more exercise but doesn't tell us what that means. Where can we find out what "healthy food" means? And getting exercise is hard because we don't have a yard. We live in an apartment. It's hard for the kids to go out and run around. We don't feel safe.

I don't like getting all this private health stuff from the school nurse about my kid. I'd rather get information from the doctor because if there is a question, the doctor can answer it.

It seems like the school is a good place for kids to be screened for a wide variety of issues from obesity to hearing and sight. All the kids are here, right? Screened at school and then notified at home with resource information. I don't trust the school screening at all.

> *It depends on how it's presented.*
>
> *It's not the school's business.*
>
> *Is the nurse capable?*

Talking about something as important to people as their children's health will always cause quite a bit of discussion. Talking about an issue such as the epidemic of childhood obesity increases the likelihood that the conversation will go in many different directions, as the causes of the epidemic are so diverse.

The questions asked of the speaker above are all valid questions. The primary issue that the speaker had to face was that the Q&A session became a debate on who should work with the parents, the schools or the physicians. This is a worthwhile debate, but the speaker needs to determine how long to let it go on and how to cut it off and change the direction of the conversation while remembering that he or she is dealing with passionate parents that care for their children.

In this case, the best advice for the speaker is:

- Be polite.
- Suggest that the parents can get more information from the organizational website.
- Suggest that the parents might direct some of their opinions to the school district or other more senior members of your organization.
- Ask another question that redirects the conversation.

The speaker may have spoken with the host before the presentation and asked that if the Q&A started to lose focus that he or she should ask a specific question, perhaps supplied by the speaker. This is a good way to redirect the situation.

Q&As can be instructive for both the audience and the speaker if they are planned well and focus is maintained. They take a little experience to manage properly, but after you have done a few of them, you will find that they might come to be the most enjoyable part of the presentation.

 Speaker's Point:

Be prepared to take notes during question and answer sessions. You often will get people that ask three or four questions at a time, so noting the questions as they are asked will help you make sure you answer the questions completely and to the best of your ability. Also, taking notes will allow you to remember any great idea audience members have.

Audience Surveys

Audience surveys are a great way of collecting specific information from a targeted audience. An organization like Teach a Kid to Fish can gather all kinds of information from contact data, social and economic data, and information related a whole host of issues regarding children's health and wellness.

There were a series of questions posed in Chapter 6 that the speaker for Teach a Kid to Fish might ask the audience as a part of the speech presentation. These questions could just as easily be made a part of an audience survey that the members of the Parent Teacher Organization are asked to fill out.

Name:

Email address:

1. *Does your child have a medical home? If your child is sick, are you able to see the doctor in a timely manner and is your child seen for a physical exam annually? What barriers are there in our community that makes it difficult to access a medical home for your child?*

2. *Does your child's doctor talk with you about your child's weight or BMI (body mass index)? Does the doctor or nurse specifically ask you about your child's nutrition, physical activity habits, and amount of screen time?*

3. *Does your child's doctor tell you or give you handouts about resources in the community for nutrition and physical activity?*

4. *What, if any, are the barriers that make it difficult to feed your child healthy foods and to be physically active?*

5. *Does your child walk to school? If not, explain what barriers exist that make it so your child does not walk to school?*

6. *What do you feel is the role of schools in the childhood obesity epidemic? Who would you like to receive information regarding your child's weight status, nutrition, and physical activity habits?*

7. *Was there anything in tonight's presentation that you would like to know more about?*

8. *Was there anything in tonight's presentation that was unclear to you?*

9. *Would you like to be put on the Teach a Kid to Fish mailing list?*

Information gathered in such a fashion can be useful to an organization like Teach a Kid to Fish. This information can be used to guide program creation as well as for fundraising. If you are creating a presentation for such an organization, consider audience surveys, as they can be quite useful in so many different ways.

Host Feedback

You might not find the opportunity to speak with your host on the day of your presentation, but host feedback can be useful. In fact, waiting several days after the presentation to contact your host to ask about how the event went will give the host a few days to hear back from some of the assembled audience.

What you will want to learn from your host will vary from situation to situation, but it can be interesting just to learn the overall impression of the audience. The host probably will be able to tell you, "Everybody thought it was a great program... though Mrs. Jones who was sitting in the last row in the back said she was disappointed that she could not hear you very well." Even this type of information is good to learn. You will be more attentive next time in making sure the elderly couple sitting in the back can hear you.

You may be interested in knowing if the organization, in this case the PTO, would like to learn more about the issue of childhood obesity. In the days after the presentation, perhaps, the PTO president might have received several calls from parents wanting to know more. It could be that a number of people could not make the presentation but heard about it from friends. They want information.

Speaker's Point:

Not all feedback is going to be positive. Not all feedback is going to be nice. Not all feedback will be delivered in the most tactful manner. Keep in mind that when you put yourself in front of the public, the responses you receive will range from glowing to embarrassing. You should take all criticism with a grain of salt, the good and the bad. You always should be polite, even to your harshest critics. You will find that all things balance out in the end.

Putting It All into Action

You might have begun this book after having been asked to prepare a speech presentation for a school election, a class project, or for the organization you volunteer with. You might have read this book because you just want to learn how to create a speech presentation and be a better speaker. The fact is, the best way to become a better speaker is just to go out and do it. This has been mentioned several times throughout this book.

If you are looking for places that will help you be a better speaker, you might join a book club, a community theater, or a local volunteer organization that you feel strongly about to act as an advocate. The book club will offer you the chance to talk about books in a relaxed setting. The community theater will allow you to speak in public in a more structured environment. The volunteer organization will offer you a subject that you feel strongly about and that you would like other people to know about. Any of these choices are a good option for someone wanting to practice their public speaking skills.

You also might consider joining a school club where you can specifically focus on the skill of public speaking. Debate team is a great way to get instruction on public speaking.

Public speaking is a skill that anyone can develop and is an important part of school. Knowing how to express yourself, whether it is in front of one person or 1000 people is important.

If you are new to public speaking or a nervous public speaker, take the steps outlined in each chapter of this book slowly and search out those places that you feel comfortable practicing with friends and local opportunities. Learning to be an effective public speaker is like learning any other skill… it just takes time, practice, and persistence.

One more thing: Your audience always wants you to succeed!

Glossary

active listening. The practice of asking questions concerning or restating what is spoken

audience. A person or group of people gathered for an event

body language. Nonverbal communication signaled by the use and movement of the body other than the voice

communication. The exchange of information

congratulatory. A laudatory or admiring word or gesture

debate. A discussion in which there is more than one of an issue discussed

diaphragm. A large muscle, located between your lungs and your abdomen, which supports breathing and speech

draft. To write

enunciate. To pronounce clearly

edit. The process of reviewing the work you have done. Editing the draft is the process of carefully going through the work to check for errors, continuity issues, missed ideas, and flow.

feedback. Response or reaction

impromptu. Extemporaneous or spontaneous

inflection. To modulate speech in such a way as to change the pitch of the pitch, tone, or enunciation of a word or the voice

informational. Knowledgeable or factual in nature

inspire. To stimulate to action

interpret. To ascribe a particular meaning to something

keynote. Main or primary

message. Communication

motivate. Inspire

outline. To lay out the main points

oral communication. The process of transmitting information verbally

orate. To speak or give a speech

persuasive. To be convincing

podium. An object that a speaker stands behind that holds a script, microphone, glass of water, or anything the speaker 1ay need to have at hand.

PowerPoint. A presentation tool capable of displaying complex graphic information

preview. A practice rehearsal with an audience

provocative. To be challenging

public speaking. Speaking to an audience on a specific topic

Q&A. Question and answer

rehearse. Practice

research. Organized study

skill. A developed ability

speech. The ability to speak; an address, lecture, or other formal communication

stage fright. The fear of performing or being in front of an audience

timing. The pace at which your presentation moves forward in a natural manner allowing for a clear natural delivery and audience interaction

toast. A salute or tribute

tone. Quality, attitude, or manner

venue. A place used for an event

Bibliography

Beebe, Steven A. and Susan J. *Public Speaking: An Audience-Centered Approach*. Boston: Pearson, 2009.

Berkun, Scott. *Confessions of a Public Speaker*. Sebastopol, California: O'Reilly Media, 2010.

Carnegie, Dale. *How to Win Friends and Influence People*. New York: Simon and Schuster, 1936.

_____. *The Quick and Easy Way to Effective Speaking*. New York: Simon and Schuster, 1962.

Dowis, Richard. The Lost Art of the Great Speech. New York: AMA Publications, 2000.

Duarte, Nancy. *slide:ology: The Art and Science of Creating Great Presentations*. Sebastopol, California: O'Reilly Media, 2008.

Esposito, Janet E. *In the Spotlight, Overcoming Your Fear of Public Speaking and Performing*. Bridgewater, Connecticut: Spotlight, LLC, 2000.

Guber, Peter. *Tell to Win*. New York: Crown Publishing, 2011.

Harvard Business Review. *Guide to Persuasive Presentations*. Cambridge, Massachusetts: Harvard Business School Publishing, 2010.

Shosky, John. *Speaking to Lead*. London: Biteback Publishing, 2010.

Simmons, Annette. *The Story Factor*. New York: Basic Books, 2001.

Zeoli, Richard. *The 7 Principles of Public Speaking*. New York: Skyhorse Publishing, 2008.

Index

O

opening statement, 88

outline, 46, 85-88, 90-93, 97-100, 102, 110, 114, 116, 118, 119, 121, 125, 218

P

persuade, 17, 34, 35, 77

persuasive, 90, 120, 13, 17, 34, 35, 145, 218, 222

persuasive speech, 13, 34

physical energy, 176, 180, 140

podium, 27, 36, 88, 114-116, 149, 159, 160, 176, 179, 180, 197-201, 142, 218

PowerPoint, 36, 46, 47, 50, 102, 105, 111, 115, 150, 160, 187, 189, 192-194, 125-127, 131, 132, 135, 137, 138, 140, 144, 219

presentations, 34-36, 41-44, 46-48, 53, 59, 60, 86, 93, 115, 116, 120, 122, 127, 133, 143, 150-153, 159, 166, 187, 190, 193, 198, 204, 205, 208, 221, 222

presenting awards/gift, 35

projection, 50, 149-152, 154, 158

Q

Q&A (question and answer) sessions, 208

S

sound equipment, 149

sources, 53, 67, 76, 80, 82

speaking fundamentals, 10

speech patterns, 172-174

stage fright, 48, 51, 52, 113, 163, 164, 173, 175, 176, 182, 184, 219

T

Timing, 51, 52, 197, 203, 204, 219

two-way communication, 201, 202

V

Venues, 147-150, 152, 153, 161, 53

video clip, 134

vision, 13, 17, 26, 36, 40, 59, 91, 103, 109, 112, 124, 141

vocal warm-ups, 51, 170, 183, 191

W

"work the room", 124, 159